Cell

by Judy Klass

SAMUEL FRENCH

FOUNDED 1830

NEW YORK HOLLYWOOD LONDON TORONTO

SAMUELFRENCH.COM

ISBN 978-0-573-69659-6   Printed in U.S.A.   #29069

**IMPORTANT BILLING AND CREDIT
REQUIREMENTS**

CELL premiered in the International Mystery Writers' Festival in Owensboro, Kentucky in June of 2008. The production was directed by Kelley Elder with the following cast and creative team:

DENNIS . . . . Steve Hudgins
MICHAEL . . . . Wes Bartlett
RODRIGUEZ . . . . Kelley Elder
JULIE . . . . Krystal Kimbley London
BYRON . . . . Marcellus Mays
EDITH . . . . Jouhanna Vasquez

Assistant Director - William B. Meloney VII
Lighting Design - Bill Peeler
Set Design - Jason Rose
Sound Design - Branson Hart
Costume Design - Chris Hart
Stage Manager - V. Aaron Brown
Properties - Sarah Lamb
Production Manager - Janice Eaves
Stage Crew - Bill Pruden, Aaron Brown, David Loney, Zach Mills
Lighting Operator - Lauren Hart

CELL has been a finalist in competitions run by Siena College, Playwrights Circle, TrapDoor Ensemble and Hinton Battle Theatre Laboratory. After it was produced in Owensboro, it was one of three plays nationwide to be nominated for an Edgar Allan Poe Award in 2009.

CHARACTERS

DENNIS – A trim, nicely dressed white man in his late thirties/early forties. Dennis is reasonable and pleasant, but he tries a little too hard.

RODRIGUEZ – A Latino police detective, thirties or forties, with a laid-back manner who nevertheless watches a suspect, such as Dennis, carefully, and invites him to talk himself into a corner.

MICHAEL – Dennis' older brother, in his late forties/early fifties. He is overweight, and both of his legs have been amputated because of his diabetes. His back hurts; he is in constant pain. A sardonic, brilliant, unfixably broken person. At times he is amused, at times bored; he is always tired, angry and bitter.

EDITH – A nurse who has known many patients and families in their private hells for several decades. A strong, kind, black Jamaican woman in her forties or fifties.

JULIE – A few years younger than Dennis, from a background similar to his, protective of him, wary of Michael.

BYRON – A black man around Michael's age. Like Michael, he is angry and bitter, and equally annoyed by pampered people like Dennis.

SETTING

In Act One, scenes One, Three, Five, Seven and Ten take place in Rodriguez's office. Two, Four, Six and Eight are flashbacks to the apartment Dennis shared with Michael. Scene Nine has Dennis and Julie walking down the street - the edge of the stage.

In Act Two, Dennis wanders in and out of flashback memories - back and forth between Rodriguez's office and the apartment Dennis shared with Michael with no real breaks except shifts in lighting.

NOTE: the play states that Michael's life ends while he is in bed. But if a director wishes to have him in his wheelchair throughout the play, dialogue can be adjusted accordingly; on page 7, instead of saying he found Michael lying there, Dennis can say "Since I found him with foam on his lips," etc. Michael can be played by an actor with legs, so long as holes are cut in his bed/wheelchair to hide them.

TIME

The present.

To Ron Reed

(SETTING: A policeman's office. **LT. RODRIGUEZ** *is questioning* **DENNIS KADMAN**.*)*

(AT RISE: They sit opposite each other, in mid-conversation. The lights are still down over the other part of the stage representing the living room of Dennis's apartment, which dominates the set. We see rumpled bedding, and perhaps a form on the high bed, or perhaps it's too dark to see anything there. Back in the brightly-lit office, **RODRIGUEZ** *is calm, and* **DENNIS** *appears angry and upset.*)*

RODRIGUEZ. And you were the one who found him?

DENNIS. Of course, I – I was practically the only one who ever saw him. It's just Michael and me, living there.

RODRIGUEZ. You took care of him, with all of his medical problems?

DENNIS. *(distracted)* What? Yes, yes, I did.

RODRIGUEZ. Are you all right, Mr. Kadman? Ready to continue?

DENNIS. *(sarcastic)* Am I all right? Well, no, actually, since you ask, not since I walked in and found my brother lying there, with foam on his lips, so –

RODRIGUEZ. I know this is a hard time for you, sir, but we do need to go over a few things here. Are you able to continue?

DENNIS. Sure.

RODRIGUEZ. You took care of your brother.

DENNIS. Yes, I did. I tried to save him from himself.

(near tears) I tried damned hard.

RODRIGUEZ. Well, that sounds like a big job, like it might take over everything in a man's life. It might get to be too much.

(waits for a response, gets none)

RODRIGUEZ. *(cont.)* Could you, uh, tell me some of what was involved in all that?

*(**DENNIS** pulls himself together.)*

DENNIS. When I was notified that Michael was in the hospital, he'd already had his legs amputated.

RODRIGUEZ. Because of –

DENNIS. Diabetes. But he takes terrible care of his health, he's never given a damn about what he eats, or exercised, or valued what he had. Ever. Brilliant kid. Talking at seven months old, my mom said. Renaissance man. Math, engineering, languages, art. He got into MIT at sixteen. And fried his brains with acid, and dropped out, and never did one *fifth* of what he was capable of doing. I mean, you can *talk* to him, and sure, you think how brilliant he is, but that's because you never met him before, it's not even a fraction, you don't have a sense of what he *used* to be!

RODRIGUEZ. Sir. I was referring to recent –

DENNIS. Oh. Sure. What was the…

RODRIGUEZ. Could you describe some of the things you did for your brother?

DENNIS. Sure. Let's see. I lift him from his cot into his wheelchair, and put him back again when he wants to lie down. I have to be home to put him on the toilet or in the bathtub. I mean, there's also a bedpan, by the bed, but, you know…There's a woman who comes and helps when I'm teaching my classes…I guess I'll have to call her. Tell her not to come tomorrow.

RODRIGUEZ. What else?

DENNIS. Well, I have to give him his pills. I shop for him, cook for him, make sure he eats right – finally! I've got him on a diet. I give him his injections of insulin, and give him his morphine –

RODRIGUEZ. *You* did?

DENNIS. Yes. A paper cup of liquid morphine, in the morning.

RODRIGUEZ. Wow. Your brother must have been in excruciating pain, for them to have allowed that.

DENNIS. It's for the pain – and the addiction, I think. He was in a methadone treatment program, at first. But without legs – he's not mobile. His friend would take him there in a wheelchair. Then they caught Michael outside trying to sell the methadone as spitback, to get money for other drugs. After that, the court and the doctors came up with the regimen of a paper cup of morphine, every morning.

RODRIGUEZ. Administered by you.

DENNIS. Or Edith, the Jamaican nurse. Whoever is there. The clinic gives me the cartridges of insulin, and the morphine I measure carefully. I keep all those things tucked away in the vestibule, and I lock that door from the inside when I'm home, and from the outside when I go out. There's no way he could have gotten at it, and taken more.

RODRIGUEZ. That's why you have all those locks installed there?

DENNIS. My brother is an addict. Was. Was a life-long addict. Chain-smoked until the hospital got hold of him, and then I got hold of him. And with his back pain and diabetes…he always wanted something. Alcohol, morphine, something to stop the pain. He said that's how he got hooked on heroin. I think he was trying to kill himself with it.

(becoming angry)

But I guess he was *always* trying to kill himself.

(lights down)

End of Scene One

Scene Two

*(The lights dim over the police station, and grow brighter over the apartment. Now, **MICHAEL** lies in bed, propped up on his elbows, coldly begging **DENNIS**, who is working to lift a stuck window, the bars of the grill pushed back from it.)*

MICHAEL. One cigarette. One cigarette a day.

DENNIS. Not in my apartment.

MICHAEL. You can supervise. You can stand over me and watch while I smoke it, and make anal, disapproving comments. Clucking noises. You can cluck like a chicken.

DENNIS. I'm sorry, but I will not have a poisonous, toxic drug stinking up my apartment.

MICHAEL. I live here too, Dennis. I'm kept in this cage, it's my "whole world," now.

DENNIS. I pay the rent.

(a beat)

It would only aggravate your addiction to nicotine.

MICHAEL. Oh, go fuck yourself with something long and sharp.

DENNIS. We could get you a nicotine patch, of course, but since you've been cigarette-free for so long…

MICHAEL. *(musing)* A red, hot poker, maybe, pulled from the coals. Shoved up your ass, like Edward II.

*(**DENNIS** has opened the window as far as it will go, shuts and locks the bars and tries to reason with **MICHAEL**.)*

DENNIS. What would be the point of smoking one cigarette a day?

MICHAEL. *(explaining the obvious to an idiot)* It would give me something to look forward to. It would give every day of my existence a few minutes of meaning.

DENNIS. I'm afraid, Mike, that you're going to have to find your meaning elsewhere. I've given you spiral note-books, the kind you've always liked. You've got pencils, you've got pens. Say the word, and I'll get you any books in the world, say the word, and you can have your own computer.

MICHAEL. Mmm.

DENNIS. Think of the fun you could have being rude to people online. And you could use it for whatever you like. Unless you turn into the Unibomber or some-thing.

MICHAEL. Mmmm.

DENNIS. *(truly hopeful)* But what I'm hoping, Mike, is that you'll use it to write the Great American Novel. Or the most amazing play in verse in the last 500 years. Or a ground-breaking treatise on physics. Or –

MICHAEL. All right, all right. You gonna start calling me Mr. Man?

DENNIS. What?

MICHAEL. Is there any novel in particular you'd care to see me crank out?

DENNIS. No. I can't begin to tell another person what to write, much less a genius.

(frustrated)

But it seems you'd rather lie there all day and watch talk shows, and sulk, and waste your brilliant mind, and feel sorry for yourself because I won't let you smoke in the apartment.

MICHAEL. Mmmm. I've changed my mind.

DENNIS. You've changed your mind?

MICHAEL. Yes. Go fuck yourself with something dull and rusty.

(lights down)

End of Scene Two

Scene three

(The lights go back up on the police office, and as **DENNIS**
rejoins **RODRIGUEZ**, *we are back where we were before.)*

RODRIGUEZ. And the last time you gave him anything was –

DENNIS. Early this morning. Just before I went out, went in
to work. If the clinic told me the wrong dosage…but
it's never been a problem before, and I gave him the
same amount as always, don't you see? Could it have
built up in his system, does that happen sometimes
with morphine? Or could he have just had a reaction
to it? They never said there was a danger.

(talking half to **RODRIGUEZ**, *and half to himself)*

They would have warned me, wouldn't they, if that were
possible? But if he somehow got that door to the vestibule open. Undid the locks, and got in there. You don't
know my brother. He's very cunning. But I still don't…
I left him tucked in, I – found him tucked in. I thought
he was asleep until I saw that…until I saw his lips.

(pursuing this new angle)

Is it possible that all this time he could maneuver without help, without the chair? Move around walking on
his *hands*? I don't think he could. He's very overweight,
I've been trying to get him to exercise…

RODRIGUEZ. Mr. Kadman, I should tell you that the pathol-
ogist has already determined that your brother died of
an overdose of heroin.

DENNIS. No, morphine.

RODRIGUEZ. No, heroin.

DENNIS. *(bewildered)* But he doesn't…how?

RODRIGUEZ. That's what we wanted to ask you, sir.

DENNIS. But I'm…I try to be so vigilant! I'd *never* let it in
the house. I examine every gift parcel, every piece of
mail he gets, first. Because mixed with the morphine
in his system, it could kill him.

RODRIGUEZ. *(writing)* You were aware of that?

DENNIS. Yes. He knows it, too. But that wouldn't stop him from –

RODRIGUEZ. Can you think of who might have supplied him with the heroin, Mr. Kadman?

DENNIS. No one! He sees me, he sees Edith. And she wouldn't, she's a competent nurse, and she wasn't there yesterday.

(thinks)

He sees Byron Carson, a wino buddy of his. The guy who took him down to the clinic that time. But now I supervise his visits. I literally frisk Byron when he comes, to prevent something like this. The two of them give me a hard time about it, I don't care. And I frisked Byron yesterday. He did not give Michael *anything*.

RODRIGUEZ. *(again writing)* Do you have an address for this man?

DENNIS. Byron? No. I don't know if he has one. Frankly, he seems like a smelly, homeless bum. To me. He mails letters for Michael. Won't let me touch them. I guess Mike's afraid I'd read what he'd written. And I wouldn't. I only examine incoming things because I have to.

RODRIGUEZ. Did Byron bring your brother anything to eat or drink?

DENNIS. No. Sometimes he brings Michael pretzels. I don't like it, but I allow it, just no beer or potato chips or candy.

RODRIGUEZ. Sounds like you're pretty tough.

DENNIS. I love my brother! Loved him.

RODRIGUEZ. You two were close, then?

(a beat)

Mr. Kadman?

DENNIS. We came close to being close a lot of the time. Or, I thought we did. It's like Charlie Brown and the football, you know? He'd hold it for me, and I'd come running up to kick it. I fell for it every time.

(lights down)

End of Scene Three

Scene Four

(Lights up over the apartment. **DENNIS**, *with his back turned to the audience, helps* **MICHAEL** *into the wheelchair, and adjusts the blanket across his upper legs.* **MICHAEL** *wheels it around.)*

DENNIS. Good. All set for the day?

MICHAEL. Oh, yeah.

DENNIS. You don't need to go –

MICHAEL. I said I'm fine.

DENNIS. *(gathering books)* Well, Edith should be here in an hour or so. And I'll be in my office until my two o'clock class, if you need to call.

MICHAEL. Yes, Mother.

DENNIS. Sure you can't think of any library books you'd like me to –

MICHAEL. No, thank you, Mother. Remember? I've got Ellen, and I've got Oprah, and I've got Jerry, and Tyra –

DENNIS. Another full day ahead, huh?

*(**HE** carefully places a scholarly journal in his bookbag.)*

MICHAEL. What's that?

DENNIS. *(too casual)* What's what?

MICHAEL. That magazine you're treating like holy parchment?

*(**DENNIS** laughs self-consciously. **HE** would very much like to show it to **MICHAEL**, but **HE** is scared.)*

DENNIS. Oh, it's nothing. I'm passing it on to Julie.

MICHAEL. Tell me what it is. Please.

DENNIS. *(embarrassed, happy, taking it out to show him)* Well, whatever, okay. It's a scholarly journal, but they're trying to lighten up their style. Print more contemporary kinds of lit crit. And they published this goofy little piece of mine.

MICHAEL. What's it on?

DENNIS. You'll laugh.

MICHAEL. I'm not laughing.

DENNIS. You'll sneer.

MICHAEL. Hey. As you say, little brother, I'm wasting my life. I do nothing with my talents all day long. How can I sneer at someone who actually accomplished something? How pathetic and transparent would that be?

(a beat)

What's it on?

DENNIS. *(handing it over, proud and shy) Oedipus Rex.* You know, publications help lead to tenure and all. But, I mean, I'm no classicist like you, Michael. I can't read Greek, obviously, I read it in translation.

MICHAEL. It's been a long time since I've had any pretensions to reading Greek. What's your thesis?

DENNIS. Well. Like I said, they want less stuffy articles, this place, they, ah, like it if you draw parallels between the classics and contemporary popular culture...

MICHAEL. They want you to link the old dead white guys to Jay-Z?

DENNIS. Well, yeah, that kind of thing. So, anyway, in this little piece, I just – I contextualize *Oedipus Rex* as the first great murder mystery. The first definitive detective story. Maybe the greatest of all time.

MICHAEL. Go on.

DENNIS. *(warming to his subject)* Well, think of the brilliant twist endings some mysteries have, beyond "the butler did it."

MICHAEL. That's where you got this title? "Sophocles Goes Beyond the Butler"?

DENNIS. Um, yeah, that's my point. I mean, a really well-constructed whodunit gives you a twist, it plants red herrings, or a whole false premise, or somehow, the solution comes out of left field.

MICHAEL. But everyone knows who sees *Oedipus Rex*, everyone who saw it in ancient times, knew the story.

DENNIS. But if one doesn't know it, it works wonderfully well. I teach it in Comp II sometimes, and I don't tell them the plot first, and most of them don't know the story, they've never heard of Freud, even –

MICHAEL. You're joking.

DENNIS. I'm not. And they're captivated! They learn the truth about who did it at the same time as the character. But as I was saying, with a really good murder mystery, they pull a complete reversal on you. For instance, you have an Agatha Christie where it turns out *everybody* did it, and Poirot doesn't turn them in because they were avenging the Lindbergh baby, basically –

MICHAEL. I know the book.

DENNIS. Or, there are some books where it turns out the victim is still alive, faked his own murder. Or, it turns out he committed suicide, and maybe the other suspects just drove him to it, and then someone moved the body. Works like that almost deconstruct the genre, they make you re-think it, a little bit. But there are no works in which the *detective himself* is the murderer.

MICHAEL. I'm afraid there is a rather long-running Agatha Christie play –

DENNIS. Yes, but he *knows* he is the murderer. The audience doesn't know it until the end, the other characters trapped with him don't know it, but *he* knows it from the beginning. But a work in which the detective investigates the crime sincerely, in the name of justice, and finds that the blood is on his own hands? Only Sophocles did that. We always want our protagonist to learn something, in any kind of literature, but that is the *only* whodunit in which the main character learns something so crucial, so personal, it destroys him. And that is why *Oedipus Rex* is, in some sense, the most perfect murder mystery every written.

(**DENNIS** *stares hopefully at* **MICHAEL,** *who considers for a minute. Then,* **MICHAEL** *slowly and sarcastically claps his hands a few times.*)

MICHAEL. Bravo, little brother. You have taken the most searing human tragedy of all time, written in blood and fire and reaching into the darkest recesses of the human psyche – and reduced it to a parlor trick.

DENNIS. *(humiliated, deflated)* I knew you would find a way to sneer.

MICHAEL. Because it's all a game to you. Scholarship, or the emotions in that play. Oedipus says:

(He recites in Greek; the capital "E" and "ei" are pronounced "a" as in "ate"; small "e" is pronounced as in "yet.")

all ei tEs akouousEs et En pEgEs di OtOn fragmos/ouk an eskomEn to mE apokleisai toumon athlion demas/ hin E tuflos te kai kluOn mEden ...

(He then repeats it in English:)

"If I could have stifled my hearing at its source/I would have done it and made all this body/A tight cell of misery, blank to light and sound:/So I should have been safe in my dark mind/Beyond external evil." A man learns a truth so unbearable, he pierces his eyes with pins ripped from his wife's clothing. His mother's clothing. But you cannot even feel the pathos of that work, and so you dissect it. You reduce the process of catharsis that Aristotle talks about, that is at the heart of witnessing any tragedy, you reduce it to a double acrostic.

DENNIS. *(defeated)* Please, may I have the journal back.

MICHAEL. I once valued being clever-clever. I was very good at it, too. Better than you, I think. Perhaps I taught it to you in your infancy, and you never outgrew it.

DENNIS. The journal. Please? It's mine. It's of no value to you.

MICHAEL. *(handing the journal over)* But nowadays, I must say, I prefer in general to watch Jerry Springer, and dream about the cigarette I am not permitted to have.

DENNIS. *(hunching into his coat)* I'll leave you to all of that.

*(**MICHAEL** calls out to **DENNIS** as he angrily heads into the vestibule:)*

MICHAEL. I hope this gets you tenure!

(The door slams.)

(lights down)

End of Scene Four

Scene Five

(The lights come up on the police office again. **DENNIS** *is standing, picking at the wall.)*

DENNIS. I was hoping that living together would bring us closer. But I can't say that it did, no.

RODRIGUEZ. And the only other two visitors to the home were this man Byron Carson, and the day nurse, Edith...

DENNIS. Singleton. Yes, and sometimes my fiancée Julie would come by.

RODRIGUEZ. Uh huh. Who, besides yourself, had a key to the apartment?

DENNIS. Edith. But today was not one of her days.

RODRIGUEZ. What was her relationship with the deceased?

DENNIS. You mean, what was it like? Good. Playful. He'd flirt with her, proposition her, say some pretty crude and inappropriate things. She'd just laugh it off.

RODRIGUEZ. And in theory, she could have come to see your brother at times when you were out, when you were not aware of it.

DENNIS. Well, yeah, I guess. I mean, she wouldn't get paid for it. But she...

*(**HE** is struck silent with thought.)*

RODRIGUEZ. Mr. Kadman?

DENNIS. She could have done it! If my brother really did overdose on heroin, she's the *only* one who could have done it.

RODRIGUEZ. And would she have a motive?

DENNIS. She told me that we should let him go, if that's what he wanted.

RODRIGUEZ. Let him go?

(lights down)

End of Scene Five

Scene Six

(Lights up on the apartment. **EDITH** *and* **MICHAEL** *are speaking.* **MICHAEL** *is calling to her from offstage, from the bathtub, behind the closed bathroom door.)*

MICHAEL *(offstage)* Hey, Edith? You still out there?

EDITH. Still here, Michael, and how can I help you?

MICHAEL *(offstage)* I was hoping you'd come in here and soap my – back, maybe? There are all these hard to reach places I can't keep clean. You'd think, with my legs out of the way, I could get 'em all, but...

EDITH. Perhaps you should be asking your brother for help.

MICHAEL. Naah, there's nothing for him in here. No boats for him to sink. And he doesn't have a woman's gentle touch.

*(***DENNIS*** has wandered into the room, from his bedroom. He finds the exchange embarrassing.)*

EDITH. Well, I'm so sorry, Michael, but I can't help you with that problem. You try soaping yourself as best you can, and you make sure you only think pure thoughts.

MICHAEL. Will that help me get clean, Edith?

EDITH. Oh, yes, I promise you.

MICHAEL. I don't think I'll ever be *really* clean and pure. No matter how much I scrub and rub.

EDITH. You do your best, Michael. I have great faith in you.

DENNIS. Ah, I'm sorry about...I guess he thinks he's being funny when he –

EDITH. It's all right, Mr. Kadman. I have harder things to handle as a nurse than your brother when he wants to be a naughty boy.

DENNIS. Well, I'm glad you take it in that spirit.

(He moves toward his room.)

EDITH. I have wanted to talk to you for some time, if you have got a moment.

DENNIS. Sure. What is it?

EDITH. I'm wondering if you have considered a change for your brother.

DENNIS. A change in what?

EDITH. In location. Have you considered a hospice, or a group home for disabled people, or a halfway house?

DENNIS. Did Mike put you up to asking me this?

EDITH. No, he did not.

DENNIS. *(angry)* Well, what exactly did he say to you that prompted this?

(She looks away.)

He asked you to get drugs for him, didn't he. What? Heroin? Other opiates? Did he ask for extra morphine from the vestibule?

EDITH. He's not a happy man, and I think he wants –

DENNIS. What did he try to get from you?

EDITH. *(flaring)* Things that would end his life. Things that he could take and not wake up afterward.

(a beat.)

DENNIS. And so *you* think that a better environment for him would be some loosely structured communal center, where a guy as devious as Michael could have his overdose smuggled in before his first *week* was over! He is the Hannibal Lector of self-destruction! Do you want to see him dead? Is that what you're saying?

MICHAEL *(offstage) (splashing)* Whoo! Sounds like one heavy-duty conference is goin' on out there! Think I'll stay in the tub for a while!

DENNIS. *(more softly)* Is that what you're saying?

EDITH. No. I don't want to see him dead.

DENNIS. Well, the only place that would keep an eye on him like I do would be a mental hospital. And do you really think he'd be happier or better off if I placed him there?

EDITH. I don't know what the best place for him would be. You might ask him what he –

DENNIS. *(incredulous)* Ask him? Ask manipulative, lying, kamikaze Mike?

EDITH. I only know how hellish it is here. For him and for you. I see what you do to each other. I'm sorry, but I can hold my tongue no longer.

DENNIS. He would be like that anywhere. Edith, he spent years doing nothing but ingesting poisons and toxins, and all he can do now is spew them back out at the rest of us.

EDITH. No. It is you and he who are toxic to each other. You create this, both of you, and it is terrible to see. Excuse me for speaking so freely. It may seem like none of my business –

DENNIS. And because it's hard, you think I should just park him somewhere, and watch him self-destruct from afar?

EDITH. Perhaps someplace else he would not try so hard to die.

DENNIS. No, I think he'd be the same. He's in withdrawal. He's in pain. He resents the loss of his legs and acts like everyone he meets is personally responsible. He won't try physical therapy, he won't exercise his mind, which is the best therapy there is. All he wants is –

EDITH. Why not let him have his cigarettes? Why not give him a drink now and then?

DENNIS. The man is ill.

EDITH. And must dying people be forbidden to ever live?

DENNIS. He's *not* dying, he's, he's got potentially *years* ahead of him. And I am going to try to see that he gets them. The court placed him in my custody – it's either here or a mental hospital, or prison.

EDITH. *(looking around at the apartment)* I wish this was more than a mental hospital or a prison cell to him. But I am not sure that it is.

DENNIS. *(irritated)* Well, the food here's better, anyhow. And I think he gets to take longer baths.

EDITH. I'm sorry to offend you, I'm sorry to make you so angry.

DENNIS. I'm not angry. I just think you should consider all aspects of a difficult situation before you offer your evaluation of it.

EDITH. *(moves to put on cardigan)* Of course, I should. But don't go thinking it's only him that I am worrying about. I think it is a crying shame what all of this does to both of you.

DENNIS. *(feeling noble)* It hasn't been "convenient" for my life. But it's simply a matter of doing whatever it takes to keep my brother alive.

EDITH. You know what I think? I think that when a person wants to go, we can argue, but after a time, they will find a way to go.

DENNIS. What do you mean "go"? Go where?

EDITH. I mean that you cannot hold him here if his heart and his spirit have already left. And the longer you hold him, the more it becomes like slow torture. Until you will not know the difference.

DENNIS. Oh, so you're saying if a person is sick and depressed and it gets expensive and inconvenient, we should just call Dr. Kevorkian and have him wheel in his machine.

EDITH. I am not saying that. But I have seen a lot of death and suffering in the time I have been a nurse, and it changed me. It changed my view. I have seen doctors let a patient go, and sign for a no code, and not resuscitate that patient. And I have felt that it was an act of human decency and mercy. If a man is in pain, if he wants to die, he will find a way to lay down and die, just by telling his body to do it.

DENNIS. Well, thanks for your cheerful prognosis. But I'm not ready to give up on him yet.

(writing check)

Now, this should cover us to the end of next week, I think. I can get him out of the bath all right by myself.

(She takes the check, studies his face for a moment. Then she calls out:)

EDITH. Michael, I'm leaving. You cooperate with your brother now.

MICHAEL *(offstage)* *(splashing)* Aw, Edith. Come in here first. I've got the water perfect now. Come join me, you'll see.

DENNIS. *(with a forced smile)* See? Signs of life.

EDITH. He talks to me much more that way around you. Because he knows it upsets you.

(She leaves, and closes the door loudly enough for **MICHAEL** *to hear.)*

MICHAEL *(offstage)* What did you say to her, Dennis? Did you tell her how close we've become, you and me? Did you promise you'd have me doing handsprings by Christmas?

DENNIS. Let me know when you want me in there to help you up.

MICHAEL *(offstage)* I'm fine. I'm completely self-sufficient in this environment. Buoyant. Flat on my back, washing up on shore. And if I want to take a leak, I don't need my little brother to help me, no sir. I just let her pour.

DENNIS. That's – more information than I really needed, Mike.

MICHAEL *(offstage)* Oh, but you know. That's how I go through life. Squirting out all the toxins I've ingested, like a squid squirts out ink.

(He begins to sing. **DENNIS** *listens for a minute, then heads into his bedroom.)*

(lights down)

End of Scene Six

Scene Seven

(Lights up on police office. Same as before.)

RODRIGUEZ. So, you think Edith killed your brother, not out of animosity, but compassion.

DENNIS. Out of what she perceived to be compassion, yes. She was comfortable with playing God. She thought that's what *I* was trying to do, by ignoring Mike's death wish.

RODRIGUEZ. And yet you trusted her to be alone with him. To give him medication and injections, everything.

DENNIS. Yes. It never occurred to me she would take things into her own hands. But Michael can be very persuasive.

RODRIGUEZ. You gave her the only duplicate copy of your key, and the freedom to come and go as she wished.

DENNIS. *(struck by a thought)* She – didn't have the only copy.

RODRIGUEZ. You just told me she did.

DENNIS. I guess I forgot. There's one other – I'm trying to be honest and helpful, Officer. This is a pretty horrible time.

RODRIGUEZ. Who else has a key?

DENNIS. I think I gave one to Julie. When we first started dating. Before I heard that Mike had surfaced and was in the hospital. You know, you give your girlfriend a set of keys in case you're stupid and lock yourself out. She's never used them.

RODRIGUEZ. As far as you know.

DENNIS. She's probably forgotten about them, also.

RODRIGUEZ. How did she and your brother get along?

DENNIS. Not well.

(after a beat, rapidly)

But she didn't do it. The whole idea of medicating somebody made her nervous, she was scared for me, having to do it –

RODRIGUEZ. What was the source of tension between them?

DENNIS. *(annoyed, protective)* Look, she didn't do it, all right? I get it, you consider this a murder investigation now. And maybe I'm your prime suspect. That's fine, I don't care, that's *your* investigation, good luck with it. But frankly, if anyone has a right to be concerned, it's me, and so I'm a little more concerned with *my* investigation. He was *my* brother. And I know I didn't do it and Julie didn't do it. Edith is still pretty hard to believe, and even Byron –

RODRIGUEZ. Mr. Kadman, as you say, in this office what goes on is *my* investigation.

DENNIS. You didn't know him.

RODRIGUEZ. Even so. I have to ask you to cooperate with me, sir, and answer the questions.

DENNIS. Fine. Go ahead. Happy sleuthing.

RODRIGUEZ. Why didn't Julie and Michael get along?

DENNIS. In time they might have…

(sighs)

It was awkward. We were just getting serious when I moved Mike in with me. He's not known for his gracious manners, and obviously, if you're sick you don't want to be around two love birds. She didn't feel good about staying over anymore. I didn't feel good about spending nights at her place. It was a real problem. We're engaged…but that didn't resolve…what to do, once we're married. I'd pitch to her maybe saving up, getting a big house in Brooklyn or Queens, and Mike would be on his own floor with a caretaker, Julie would practically never see him…she didn't really go for it.

RODRIGUEZ. But now the problem is solved.

DENNIS. *(steely)* I guess. But not by Julie. She's an honest, decent person.

RODRIGUEZ. But the man wanted to die.

(a beat)

Did they ever chat together, alone?

DENNIS. Yeah, I'd make dinner, leave them to get to know each other. It didn't go too well. Mike's got a strange sense of humor. Julie couldn't really get into it, I guess, like Edith did.

RODRIGUEZ. Was Michael living with you when you became engaged?

DENNIS. *(rising, bothered by memories)* Julie and I went out that night.

RODRIGUEZ. But it was after he moved in?

DENNIS. Yes.

(lights down over police station)

End of Scene Seven

Scene Eight

(DENNIS steps back into the world of the apartment. MICHAEL lies on his cot, watching DENNIS move around, tidying the apartment. He sets to work on the floor with a broom and dustpan.)

MICHAEL. My, how clean everything looks! Big date tonight, huh?

DENNIS. Um, yes.

MICHAEL. Why's she coming here first? Couldn't she just meet you at the restaurant? Wouldn't that be more pleasant, all around?

DENNIS. She's bringing her houseplant. For me to water while she's away next week. So, I thought I'd make the apartment look fit to be seen.

MICHAEL. I guess you'd rather not have me lying around naked, showing off my bedsores, then? They're kind of runny right now.

DENNIS. If you could refrain from doing that, that would be great, Michael. I would appreciate that.

(He puts away the broom and dustpan. Goes over to a small table and starts sorting through loose papers — looking them over and throwing some away.)

MICHAEL. Where you taking her?

DENNIS. Ponte Vecchio. An Italian place.

MICHAEL. I figured. From the name.

DENNIS. Well, that's where I'm taking her.

MICHAEL. *(with sarcastic heartiness)* But why not eat in? You cook such fine Italian food! We could all play charades, afterward.

DENNIS. *(serious)* I'd like to spend an evening with you and Julie sometime, Mike. Playing charades, Scrabble, whatever you like. I'm sure you'd beat the pants off of both of us. I think you and Julie might surprise yourselves by hitting it off. But for tonight – the restaurant's a little more romantic. Besides, this place makes an amazing putanesca.

MICHAEL. Putanesca. You like to order that just so you can say the name out loud. It makes you feel rude, and wild, and bohemian.

DENNIS. No. I actually like the dish.

MICHAEL. Have you ever done anything rude and wild and bohemian, Dennis? In your shabby, earnest, careful little life?

DENNIS. I suppose –

MICHAEL. What?

DENNIS. I'm kinda busy right now, Mike.

MICHAEL. Can't think of anything, huh? Not a single impulsive, unhealthy, immoral action? Not a filthy word uttered? Throughout your clean-cut, middle-aged adolescence? Never put down that *SAT Review Book* even once? No? Just sweated over it in your little yellow alligator shirt and your chinos and penny loafers? Didn't you talk back to the milk monitor once, in second grade? When you thought no one else could hear? Stop tidying a minute, baby brother, and answer me.

DENNIS. *(nettled)* I guess you were so good at being rude and doing wild things that I left it all to you, Mike. I didn't try to compete. Anyhow, wasn't that what your generation was all about?

MICHAEL. My generation?

DENNIS. Your g-g-generation, yeah. Slamming doors, giving the finger to your parents, throwing tantrums. Isn't that what the Sixties was? An extended tantrum?

MICHAEL. So. That's how you see the anti-war movement and the civil rights movement: as a temper tantrum.

DENNIS. Not completely, not everybody involved. But most of you, jumping on the bandwagon, yeah. For every Freedom Rider who went down South and took real risks, for every conscientious objector who went to prison for his beliefs, there were a million more of you making peace signs and smoking doobies and growing your hair all stringy, and grokking water, and being wild and crazy and nonconformist in exactly the same way. And there was a tendency among Baby Boomers to glorify their adolescent tantrums as political statements or spiritual experiences, yes.

MICHAEL. Gee. It sounds like you have some issues here, Dennis.

DENNIS. You'd get high and drop out, and strum guitars, and wallow like walruses in the mud at Woodstock. And that was supposed to save lives or help minorities?

MICHAEL. Well, shit. At least we *had* a youth. You're jealous because you never did. You were planning your careers back when it was "Morning in America." You went directly from infancy to cautious, corporate –

DENNIS. No, you're right. In some sense, GenXers didn't have any youth. There wasn't endless money to spend and endless time to play when we were in our teens. You couldn't go frolic in the woods or on a commune or set out to "find America" or expand your head for three years and know that Mommy and Daddy would always foot the bill. You had to live in the real world. Or I did, anyway. It's easy to turn into a "bread head" and worry about an education and a decent job when adulthood involves actual responsibilities.

MICHAEL. Naaah. Sorry, I'm not buying it. Face it, Dennis, you're just humorless and boring and completely straight. In any given situation, you're going to make the safest choice –

DENNIS. *(flaring)* Was taking *you* in the safest choice? Was this the easy way out?

MICHAEL. I didn't say you take the *easy* choice. You'll roll your rock up the mountain for years with plodding, unimaginative persistence. And get ploughed by it, and start all over again. But, yeah. It's safer to take me in than to admit you hate my guts. That there is *no* connection, *no* relationship between us. That all those platitudes about "family" you mouth are so much horse shit. That the honorable thing is to *let me die*, like I want. It would take courage to challenge your assumptions and admit those things. You'd be on unfamiliar terrain. It's much safer to just pat yourself on the back over everything you've done for me instead, and impose your life-style on me, and feel sorry for yourself when the bad man is mean to you.

DENNIS. *(angry, near tears)* You know, it's perfect that you equate persistence with a lack of imagination. Since you have never finished *one* thing you've started, in your entire life. How many unfinished stories, and novels, and experiments? How many causes and religions did you try on? What are you gonna be this week, Mike? An astronaut? A fireman? And whatever your theory or the project of the moment was, how *proud* Mom and Dad were! How full of hope, how *sure* you'd succeed! And then you'd flake out, drop out, and break their hearts again, kick them in the teeth again when they begged you to follow through.

(furious)

When you experimented on yourself and cooked your brain with every goddamned chemical you could get your hands on, with a new personality every week, *they* were the ones who really suffered. Just like your spaced-out, groovy friends made their families suffer. And I just sat on the sidelines and watched. And when the bunch of you were done being Kerouac or Peter Fonda or Timothy Leary, or Jane Fonda, so many of you Boomers – not you, of course – settled down and became conservative yuppie scum. Still feeling righteous and somehow bohemian and daring, all the while. You, on the other hand, just became an apolitical bum. But I watched it all happen, and I was not impressed. The bunch of you just feel so damn special, like whatever age you are, you're the first, you're the best – when it's just that there are *more* of you, so advertisers cater to you, all the films about young people when I was growing up had to be set in the Fifties or Sixties, except for putrid John Hughes films, otherwise we were invisible…Anyway. Whatever. Now you know what my issues are.

MICHAEL. Well, I'm glad that it's nothing personal.

(a beat)

I *like* you like this, Dennis. All fiery and feisty. What's the occasion?

*(**DENNIS** turns and goes back to his cleaning.)*

DENNIS. No occasion. Sometimes I can metabolize your goading better than other times, that's all.

MICHAEL. No, but you've been short-tempered and tied up in knots all day. Trouble in the relationship?

DENNIS. Nope. Thanks for asking.

MICHAEL. It must be getting serious. If you're taking her to some fancy restaurant for romantic putanesca. Think you might actually score?

DENNIS. What? Michael, how many nights have I slept at – forget it, Mike, yeah, that must be it.

MICHAEL. Now, now, I'm just teasing. If you've already gotten lucky, and you're so nervous – I figure either she's pregnant, or tonight you're gonna pop the question.

*(**DENNIS** moves to another part of the room.)*

That's it, isn't it. Don't try to hide from me, baby brother, I can read you like a book. This is a pretty important day for you, huh. A pretty momentous occasion.

DENNIS. Yeah, it is, Mike. Or it potentially could be. So, please don't –

MICHAEL. Please don't what?

DENNIS. Nothing.

MICHAEL. Please don't trample on something fragile and beautiful? Please don't soil it? Defile it?

DENNIS. Well, please don't *try* to. I don't know why I'm asking, it'll only make you worse. But in my case, you have the ability to ruin things simply by wanting to ruin them, and so I wish – I wish you wouldn't.

MICHAEL. You wish I wouldn't *want* to ruin your life?

DENNIS. Yeah. That's what I wish.

(looks down)

Geez, I've gotten myself so dirty, let me just run a comb through my hair, wash my face…

(He wanders into the bathroom. **MICHAEL** *listens to the sink running.)*

*(***DENNIS*** *emerges from the bathroom, his hair combed down.)*

MICHAEL. May I tell you how you look?

DENNIS. Sure, Michael. How do I look?

MICHAEL. Nervous. But terrific. You look handsome. Sharp. If you asked me to marry you tonight, I'd say yes.

DENNIS. Seriously?

MICHAEL. Seriously. Go ahead and try it.

DENNIS. Well, I don't know, I mean, this shirt, it's not too –

MICHAEL. It's a nice shirt, and you look great.

DENNIS. Well, thanks.

MICHAEL. Of course, look who you're asking.

DENNIS. You used to be a pretty romantic guy, Michael. When you were in high school… you wrote some amazing romantic love poetry.

MICHAEL. You read my notebooks?

DENNIS. You let me read some. All those villanelles. You know, I've tried to write villanelles a few times in my life. Excruciatingly awful. Not even close. I don't know any modern poets with anything like your assurance, your freshness with that form. Have you ever published –

MICHAEL. Nope. And I burned all those notebooks a long time ago.

DENNIS. *(upset)* You're not serious.

MICHAEL. A man on the move can only lug his grubby adolescent poetry notebooks with him to so many places. Eventually, they wind up on the fire.

(**DENNIS** *sits on the edge of the cot.*)

DENNIS. God, that's a shame. I remember one…I wish I could remember the whole thing. Maybe if I try, I could write it down…

MICHAEL. Please don't.

DENNIS. You told me you were on acid when you wrote it. It had a strange quality, I'll say that much. The repeating lines were "Your current courses quicksand through my veins," and "The surge becomes a singing in the vines."

MICHAEL. God, how hideous. Why would you remind me of something like that? You just asked me to be gentle with you.

DENNIS. *(concentrating, reciting)* "Each cord that interweaves and intertwines,

And with the pulse of oxygen expands…

Your current courses quicksand through my veins."

MICHAEL. Please stop.

DENNIS. "The breathing of the tendrils, when it rains

The wires that the waterflow commands:

The surge becomes a singing – "

MICHAEL. I said stop it.

DENNIS. "In the vines." It was so strange and beautiful. But I bet you could write just as well without the drugs. I know you could.

MICHAEL. I was a clever lad, then, no doubt about it. A bored, precocious, alliterating zithead.

DENNIS. You were amazing.

MICHAEL. And you spent years reciting that drivel to yourself, did you?

DENNIS. Who did you write all those love poems to?

MICHAEL. Nobody you know.

DENNIS. You could have been Byron. I mean, you *were* Byron, Shelley and Keats, you *were*.

MICHAEL. Byron is a friend of mine of whom you disapprove.

DENNIS. I mean the real Byron. You could have been anything. You still could.

MICHAEL. How about you, Dennis? Write any love poetry?

DENNIS. Me? Hell, I'm no romantic poet –

MICHAEL. You're shaping up to be a pretty romantic guy. All this fire and passion I didn't even know about.

DENNIS. Don't mock me, please.

MICHAEL. There's nothing I can say at this point that you won't take as mockery, is there?

DENNIS. Probably not.

MICHAEL. You just impressed me by telling me off. You want to connect, you want to have a real conversation. I thought that's what we're trying to do, here.

DENNIS. I hope that's what we're trying to do.

MICHAEL. So, show me some of your poetry. Do you send it out?

DENNIS. What? No!

MICHAEL. Hey, you were just scolding me for not sending mine out. So, let's see it. Got any on you?

(DENNIS *glances down, then away.*)

Sonofabitch, I believe you do. Were you planning to propose with it?

DENNIS. I won't have the nerve…I probably won't even have the nerve to ask her…Oh, God, Michael, please don't –

MICHAEL. I won't tell her what you're up to. You can dig your own grave. Now, hand over the poem.

DENNIS. No.

MICHAEL. Hand it over, or I'll blab as she comes through the door: "He's popping the question, he's popping the question!"

DENNIS. *(horrified)* Michael!

MICHAEL. However, if you let me read your poem, I'll behave perfectly.

(DENNIS *considers. He actually very much wants* MICHAEL *to read it.*)

DENNIS. Basic blackmail. I guess I have no choice.

(He pulls a piece of paper, folded over, out of his pocket, and hands it to his brother. **MICHAEL** *opens it.)*

MICHAEL. No, you do not.

(He sees the diamond ring taped to the paper.)

My God. That's an original approach. Dispense with the box, and scotch tape the ring –

DENNIS. I didn't like the boxes the jewelry store had.

MICHAEL. You've obviously put some thought and care into this.

DENNIS. *(hiding head in hands)* Read the poem, get it over with.

MICHAEL. All right.

(reads:)

As I reached out to touch your hair
I spanned the chasm of the night
And gulfs of silence, on a dare;
I launched this pale bird, that it might
Alight upon a strange address,
Find harbor on an alien shore,
Defying years of loneliness:
My only refuge, metaphor.
At long last, Noah launched a dove,
And off it flew in search of land,
Returning with a sprig of love:
And so I reach to take your hand.

DENNIS. *(puts out hand for the paper)* Okay, now go ahead and mock, get it over with, and then let me get ready for my date.

MICHAEL. Just a moment, I'm considering this. Do you have time to run off another copy before she gets here?

DENNIS. Why?

MICHAEL. Well, you might want to change a few...I mean, it's good, and it's right for the purpose. But why start

off in the past tense? Wouldn't it be cleaner to say "As
I *reach* out to touch your hand/I *span* the chasm of the
night"?

DENNIS. There was –

MICHAEL. Yes?

DENNIS. A moment on one of our first dates. I brushed
back the hair from her face…I think she'll remember
it.

MICHAEL. I see, a private, shared memory, that's why you
want that part in past tense. Mmmm. I'm not sure
about "Alight upon a strange address."

DENNIS. I know.

MICHAEL. Maybe "Alight amidst…" No, that's no good,
either. "Alight before…" No.

DENNIS. That's the problem.

MICHAEL. But it's a nicely crafted poem. The image of the
dove returning with the olive branch is lovely.

DENNIS. *(shy, pleased)* Thank you.

MICHAEL. I suppose you couldn't go with iambic pentam-
eter – you'd feel called upon to write a sonnet. This
meter you're using has a nice "SamIamish" quality to
it, actually.

DENNIS. SamIamish?

MICHAEL. *(pretending to read again)*
Would you, could you in a boat?
Would you, could you with a goat?
I do not like green eggs and ham,
I do not –

DENNIS. *Enough!*

(**HE** *snatches the paper back, and crumples it, tears it
accidentally.*)

MICHAEL. What, I said boat, I was trying to keep your
Noah's ark motif. But you're so rough! Love poetry
has to be handled gently. Run, go print it out again.

(DENNIS pries the ring off the paper, and puts it into his pocket, loose. He crumples the poem further, and throws it in the wastepaper basket.)

DENNIS. Never mind, it's ruined. I asked you not to. I suppose that's why you did it.

MICHAEL. And I asked you not to recite *my* adolescent drek. But you just couldn't help yourself.

DENNIS. It won't happen again.

MICHAEL. I remember the pleasure of being a precious, clever lad. Of imagining that you are making love to your subject, or to your muse, and you never realize all the while that it's an act of masturbation.

DENNIS. Any attempt at something constructive or beautiful or personal, I guess that's how you'd see it, now, huh?

MICHAEL. You have a great facility with words, Dennis. Are you aware of the different meanings of the word "facility"?

DENNIS. I wish I could find a facility that would take you.

MICHAEL. Very good. But I mean are you aware of the root, when we speak of a person having a *facility* with words?

DENNIS. You're saying it comes too easy. Actually, that poem didn't, but whatever.

MICHAEL. Are you aware of the etymological relationship between the words "facility" and "facile"?

DENNIS. Yes, I guess I sort of was, Michael. But thank you for pointing it out to me.

MICHAEL. It's cleverness and prettiness and pat, literary games covering anything honest with a layer of shellack. You're pouring out your deepest, most honest, most *sensitive* feelings – but you still manage to add the little flourishes, and say "look Ma, no hands!"

DENNIS. I guess that's all poetry or any form of art is to you, Mike. I guess that's why you don't create anything anymore.

MICHAEL. I guess so. Of course, in your case it's all so *nice*. And sentimental. And cute. And safe. Like those loafers you used to wear, and those John Hughes movies you repudiate, as though they weren't the sum total of what you are.

DENNIS. Great. Thanks.

MICHAEL. The soul-wrenching angst of Ferris Bueller.

(*The doorbell chimes.*)

DENNIS. (*resigned*) That's great, Mike. So, go ahead now, ruin the rest of it.

MICHAEL. I have no idea what you mean.

(**DENNIS** *unlocks the door, and goes out into the vestibule.*)

(*In a moment, he returns with* **JULIE,** *who is dressed up a bit also. She is carrying a large, fussy houseplant.*)

DENNIS. Here, let me take that into the kitchen, that's where there's the most light. Meanwhile, I'm sure Michael has things he wants to tell you.

MICHAEL. Who, me?

DENNIS. (*striding out of the room with the plant*) Take your best shot.

(**JULIE** *is left to awkwardly exchange glances with* **MICHAEL.**)

JULIE. How are you, Michael?

MICHAEL. Wretched, in pain, and jonesing for sex or drugs. How are you, Julie?

JULIE. Oh, I'm doing okay.

MICHAEL. I hear you're going away.

JULIE. Colorado. Academic conference.

MICHAEL. What fun. Why not take Dennis along? Couldn't he get leave?

JULIE. I asked him, he won't leave you.

MICHAEL. Ah, what a shame. Julie, if a man were a clever writer, and he wrote a poem describing himself as an oozing bedsore, since he is in fact covered with oozing bedsores, would you consider that an analogy, or a sustained metaphor? I ask because you are an English teacher, like my brother, and you understand the ways of clever writers.

JULIE. Well, gee. I don't know. I guess I'd have to see the poem, Michael. Who knows, maybe I'd just call it a self-portrait. Or –

(less hostile)

I guess I'd really have to see it, to form an opinion.

*(**DENNIS** re-enters, still agitated and upset, and hunches into a coat.)*

DENNIS. Well, let's go. I take it that Michael has filled you in completely?

JULIE. Only about oozing bedsores.

DENNIS. Oh? Oh. Well, let's try to get away from him, then.

MICHAEL. Quickly, quickly!

*(**DENNIS** opens the door, and hustles **JULIE** into the vestibule. Then he turns back.)*

DENNIS. But, Michael, I'll have my cell phone on, so if you –

MICHAEL. Get out of here, you crazy kids.

DENNIS. Well – thank you. For merely being disgusting, in the end.

MICHAEL. The least I could do. Now, please leave.

*(**DENNIS** closes the door to the vestibule, and locks the locks on the other side of the door. Lights down over apartment.)*

End of Scene Eight

Scene Nine

(**DENNIS** and **JULIE** *walk along a city street together, later that evening. Traffic noises can be heard.* **DENNIS** *is wired, and very, very stressed.*)

JULIE. Well.

DENNIS. Well?

JULIE. That was one of the strangest meals I've ever had.

DENNIS. *(rapid, nervous)* Yeah, I was worried about that tortellini in brodo, I mean, I've never tried it, but I know they can be uneven there, that's why I play to their strength, which is putanesca, I should have warned you –

JULIE. You did.

DENNIS. I did, but I guess I should have warned you – more forcefully.

JULIE. The food was fine, Dennis. The meal was strange because… What is going on with you?

DENNIS. *(defensive)* What do you mean?

JULIE. I mean you keep zoning out while I'm talking to you, then you're giving me a discourse on Italian wine, then you're dismissing the work of all these great writers, just to impress me –

DENNIS. I'm just – jumpy.

JULIE. I see that. Did you have a fight with Michael?

DENNIS. Well, of course, he saw we were going out, he had to mess with me…was he very rude to you?

JULIE. Not really – I just need to not take the bait. But what did you guys fight about?

DENNIS. Baby Boomers vs. GenXers.

JULIE. Oh boy.

DENNIS. We've never really gotten into the whole generational thing before, so it was interesting, actually –

JULIE. And would he agree with me that there is no such thing as generations, as such, and that this whole obsession of yours is kind of perplexing and sad?

DENNIS. Um – no. No, I don't think he would agree with you. I think he does think very much in terms of generations, most Boomers do. They just think that theirs is the only one that matters.

JULIE. Okay. Well, look, let's not get into a whole –

DENNIS. I just would like to understand better how you felt about all of that, growing up. Seeing their images everywhere. That never bothered you? All the Vietnam films, and on TV, "The Wonder Years"?

JULIE. I didn't watch that much TV.

DENNIS. You never saw all those sit-coms, with them playing the parents, and the kids our age were supposed to learn through being humiliated? We were just these hapless little Cosby kids handing straight lines to our elders!

JULIE. Maybe, but so what, who cares? Don't you see that you generalize about this stuff to the point of absurdity, and you don't even acknowledge that it's not about this whole group of people you keep labeling, it's all about you and your brother –

DENNIS. No! They were the ones who said "Never trust anyone over thirty!" They were the ones who said "Hope I die before I get old," not me!

JULIE. Dennis, there is no "they."

DENNIS. You never read the magazine articles when we were in high school about a new threat called AIDS? And they'd say: "Maybe it's not a bad thing that we all have to settle down and be monogamous, now, after our swinging young years." Just as you and I entered our teens? That didn't make you want to hunt them down and kill every last one of them?

JULIE. So, now you're blaming HIV on a whole demographic?

DENNIS. In a way, yes. They partied until it got messy and nasty, and by the time we showed up, all we could do was pick our way through the debris.

JULIE. I can't tell if you're serious, or teasing me, or what.

Whenever you launch into this…"Baby Boomer," what does it even mean?

DENNIS. It's anyone born after World War II who can remember "where they were" when Kennedy was shot.

JULIE. Oh, for pity's sake!

DENNIS. I'd include anyone who can remember the shooting of Bobby Kennedy too. They think like Boomers.

JULIE. See, I like to think that you're joking, or half-joking. That deep down, you know that people are *people*. I like to think you're too smart to write off whole groups based on their ethnic background or the country they come from –

DENNIS. That's not what I'm doing –

JULIE. Or something equally arbitrary and bigoted. And when I see you interact with individual people from different generations, colleagues, older students, you're fine, and you *do* seem to see them as people. But then when you go off on this topic, and you won't even acknowledge what's at the core of it, it really just leaves me turned off, and kind of – bewildered.

DENNIS. I'm sorry.

JULIE. And you haven't done it for a while… You sorta know better now, around me. But I guess I should have expected it, after that dinner. Because – this is what I mean. You've just been so hyper, and going off on these tangents, and lecturing me, and snapping at me –

DENNIS. You're right, you're right, I'm sorry.

JULIE. Then you're apologizing to me up and down.

DENNIS. I'm sorry.

JULIE. I don't *need* you to be sorry! I need you to tell me what's going on.

DENNIS. I'm just…insane.

JULIE. Yes, we know that. That's a given. But why tonight, especially? Why is the atmosphere between us this – charged? Why are you all hyper, and wary of me? Was it something he said to you that really hurt, or something you're feeling about me, or me and you – because I can take it, and I'd rather know than try to guess. Dennis? Come on. You can tell me. I'm not the enemy. I'm your friend. You know? Friend?

(She takes his hand. He looks at their clasped hands.)

DENNIS. Are you…my *friend*, or are you my friend?

JULIE. Is this a trick question?

DENNIS. *(fumbles in pocket)* Are you…

(finds ring, slips it on her finger)

Are you this kind of friend?

*(**SHE** looks at the ring. He looks away.)*

JULIE. Um.

DENNIS. I'm asking…I don't want to be facile, Julie, I'm not trying to be cute, I'm not trying anything, I'm asking –

JULIE. Yes.

DENNIS. Yes?

JULIE. Yes.

DENNIS. *(stunned)* Yes.

JULIE. *(tapping him on the shoulder)* Dennis?

DENNIS. Yes?

(He looks at her. She kisses him. He kisses her back, and puts his arms around her.)

JULIE. So, it's going to be all right now.

DENNIS. I meant to ask during dinner, I'm sorry, I –

JULIE. Ssshhhh.

DENNIS. I had my lines all worked out, I had a clever-clever little poem –

JULIE. Let's hear it.

DENNIS. No, written.

JULIE. Where?

DENNIS. It's not…it wasn't the way to go.

JULIE. Well, you can show me later.

DENNIS. I'd rather not.

JULIE. Okay. This is nice, too.

DENNIS. Yeah. Yeah, this is nice.

JULIE. That was even one reason I thought of, during dinner. For why you were so nervous.

DENNIS. You knew I was going to ask?

JULIE. It flashed through my mind. Or that you were going to break up with me, or you'd just knocked over a bank or killed a man or something, and you didn't know how to tell me.

DENNIS. I just didn't want to do it in a way that was – insincere. Or seemed like I was showing off. I wanted it to be about you and me, not some saccharine scene out of a John Hughes movie, some blow-dried Estevez coming on to Molly Ringwald or something, and that adorable little poem...

(She has a realization, and steps back.)

JULIE. What did he say about it? Michael. When you showed it to him.

DENNIS. I didn't –

JULIE. *(angry)* What did he say? Did he give it a two out of ten?

DENNIS. Julie, I didn't even want to tell him, he saw me getting ready to go out, he can read me –

JULIE. What did he *say*?

DENNIS. That it was...facile. And precious.

JULIE. Is it still on your computer?

DENNIS. Yeah.

JULIE. I'd like to see it. Since it was meant for me. And I'd like you to reconstruct for me how you planned to propose. So I'll know what the evening might have been like.

(pause)

Dennis, I love you, and I want to marry you. And we're engaged, and I am your fiancée.

(takes his hand again)

JULIE. *(cont.)* But you know – I hope – that we cannot get married with all of this looming over us.

DENNIS. With Mike?

JULIE. You, me and Mike don't add up to a home, to a family. You and Mike together don't even add up to family.

DENNIS. Look, I can't – don't you have friendships or family relationships you can't explain to other people? That people outside can't begin to understand?

JULIE. You're not hearing him. He *hates* you.

DENNIS. Look. There were moments tonight...we came so close...There are moments when we...

JULIE. He lets out line, and plays with you, and then he reels you in a little, *almost* all the way, but only so he can get his harpoon ready. He eviscerates you, Dennis. It's the only pleasure he's got left, and he's got you fascinated by it, and you can't even see it.

DENNIS. He's capable of other pleasures. He has other talents and interests, and sometimes I see them stirring –

JULIE. Maybe he just wants to rest. And you're shouting "Do not go gentle" at him, and you need him to fight, when he doesn't want to, and you need his parental benediction –

DENNIS. He's not my parent, I know that. He's my brother.

JULIE. He's something much more sick and twisted than that to you.

DENNIS. That can be pretty sick and twisted.

(Pause. They regard each other.)

JULIE. You and I cannot be together until you free yourself from his hold on you. You must put him in an institution.

DENNIS. He'd be dead in a week.

JULIE. That may be, and it's too bad, but it's not your

problem.

DENNIS. How can you say that?

JULIE. Look at the shadow he casts over us! Look at what he has done to this evening. Look at how he sabotages every dream of yours, how he makes everything ugly and hopeless.

DENNIS. You don't have to see it that way.

JULIE. He is an absolute sadist. And there's no one else he can really hurt, so he goes to work on you. You're an experiment to him. You're not a person, you're a one-cell organism trapped on a microscope slide.

DENNIS. He's the one who's trapped.

JULIE. He's got a scientist's detachment. He doesn't really feel anything, except physical pain. And some kind of abstract pleasure at the pain he causes you.

DENNIS. You're the one who's making this ugly now, please!

(more gently)

Please.

JULIE. *(squeezes his hand)* I want to be with you, Dennis. But I think you have to choose. Between the past and the future.

*(**DENNIS** walks away, hands jammed in his pockets.)*

(calls after him) I really hope you choose the future!

(lights down)

End of Scene Nine

Scene Ten

(Lights up on DENNIS *and* RODRIGUEZ.*)*

RODRIGUEZ. I'd have to say again…she had a pretty strong motive.

DENNIS. I suppose. But she didn't do it.

RODRIGUEZ. Okay. So. This Edith. Her motive is not as clear. Nothing as personal. But if she has strong feelings about mercy killings, like you say –

DENNIS. She does.

RODRIGUEZ. Then, it's possible. But from everything I'm hearing, the strongest suspect remains…you.

DENNIS. *(rubs his forehead)* Oh, for God's sake.

RODRIGUEZ. Tell me again how you found the body.

DENNIS. We're wasting time.

RODRIGUEZ. I don't think so. Tell me again.

DENNIS. I unlocked the door. I entered the apartment. Mike was tucked up on his cot, just as I left him. His eyes were open. I spoke to him, he didn't respond. He seemed very still. I went over, I saw the froth on his lips…and I saw it wasn't him anymore.

RODRIGUEZ. What do you mean?

DENNIS. I've never seen a body before. But you could tell. It wasn't Michael. Just – an untenanted house.

RODRIGUEZ. And how did you spend the day up until then?

DENNIS. Went in early, to finish grading papers, then teach. Lunch with Julie, and then I came home.

RODRIGUEZ. You were first at your office at what hour?

DENNIS. I don't know. Nine-thirty. Bill Harper shares my office, he was there too, he could tell you.

RODRIGUEZ. Mmm. But according to the coroner, you could have already done it.

DENNIS. What?

RODRIGUEZ. The fatal dose of heroin could have been administered very early in the morning.

DENNIS. No one was with him very early in the morning except for me. And I did not give Michael any heroin. I think I'd remember that. Don't you?

RODRIGUEZ. Well, but the mind can play tricks on us.

DENNIS. Oh, for God's sake!

RODRIGUEZ. *(soothing, reasonable, understanding)* When we're under pressure, day after day. You know, sometimes we love someone, but the love gets mixed up with other things. Sometimes it's overwhelming, taking care of someone who's sick, and addicted. Sometimes the person messes with us, and *messes* with us, and finally we snap. Sometimes their suffering is terrible, terrible to see, and they want something they shouldn't have – and we give in. It's not premeditated. It's not even a deliberate, conscious act, exactly. We find it hard to admit to ourselves we've done it. It doesn't exist in our mind as a memory, so much as…

DENNIS. Could we get serious, here?

RODRIGUEZ. *(still mild, sympathetic)* I am very serious, Mr. Kadman. And all these issues, all the things weighing on your mind, and your brother's terrible condition, his eagerness to go, it might not seem like murder, and it wouldn't be prosecuted like that. People would take the situation into account.

DENNIS. I don't believe this.

RODRIGUEZ. I'm saying that with all your mixed feelings about your brother, and his pain, and his desire for heroin, and all these people in your life telling you to let him die –

DENNIS. And me telling them to go to Hell! For Christ's sake! There's a *murder* here to solve, and we're wasting time!

RODRIGUEZ. You keep saying that.

DENNIS. *(exasperated)* But you're not hearing anything that I'm telling you! For crying out loud! Are you blind or deaf? This is the best the NYPD has to offer? A guy saying to me maybe you injected your brother with heroin, Dennis, and you just forgot? There's a murderer on the loose, okay? It's not me, it's not Julie, do you want to solve this thing or not?

RODRIGUEZ. I want to solve this thing, Mr. Kadman. I'm sorry if you don't like the way I run my investigation.

(DENNIS realizes how rude he sounds.)

DENNIS. Look, I'm sorry. I shouldn't talk to you that way. To you, I'm a suspect, I understand. But since I'm me, I know that I didn't do it, you see that? *And I want to know who killed my brother.*

RODRIGUEZ. So, let's go over it again.

(lights down)

End of Act One

ACT TWO

Scene One

(*SETTING:* **RODRIGUEZ***'s office, an hour later.*)

(*AT RISE:* **DENNIS** *sits alone, glancing over the items on the detective's desk.*)

(**RODRIGUEZ** *enters, carrying a large sandwich. He waves to* **DENNIS** *in a friendly way.*)

RODRIGUEZ. You want half?

DENNIS. No, I'm okay.

RODRIGUEZ. Sure? I don't think you've eaten in a while. This is huge, I can't finish this.

(**HE** *settles down to eat it.* **HE** *remains casual – slouching on his desk or sprawling on his chair – while* **DENNIS** *remains tense and formal.*)

DENNIS. No, really, I'm good.

RODRIGUEZ. We always order out from that deli, A Cut Above. You know it?

DENNIS. No. I mean, I pass by, but I've never gone in there.

RODRIGUEZ. Well, you should check it out. Very nice sandwiches. The salad bar isn't so good. They should play to their strengths, and just do the old-fashioned deli stuff.

DENNIS. I'm sorry I flipped out at you before. I'm sorry I was so rude. I understand that you're just doing your job.

RODRIGUEZ. S'okay.

DENNIS. I just really want to find out what happened, you know? Actually, I can't believe that I'm so calm. I feel like I'm detached, like a balloon. Full of helium, and floating.

RODRIGUEZ. Don't worry about it, you're just in shock. It's a good thing, it's a form of self-protection. You're in a kind of a cocoon of disbelief.

DENNIS. Yeah. This is all preposterous, in a way. The idea that he's dead.

RODRIGUEZ. *(munching)* So, you've been sitting here admiring the decor?

DENNIS. Yeah.

(indicates sign on desk)

T. Rodriguez. What's the "T" for?

RODRIGUEZ. Tomás. But you can call me Tommy.

DENNIS. Okay.

(indicating framed photograph on desk)

That your family?

RODRIGUEZ. Yeah.

DENNIS. They look nice. Your wife looks – cheerful. And those are nice-looking kids.

RODRIGUEZ. Thank you.

DENNIS. Did you always want to be a cop?

RODRIGUEZ. Always. Like everybody else at first, but I just never stopped.

DENNIS. And were you always a detective? Or did you start out as, like, a cop on the beat?

RODRIGUEZ. I was a cop on the beat for five years. I don't like desk work, you know, clerical work. It was a good job for a young man starting out, I got to hang out in my old neighborhood.

DENNIS. Is it weird being, like, a Latino cop in the NYPD?

RODRIGUEZ. *(mouth full)* Weird how?

DENNIS. Well, do other cops give you a hard time?

RODRIGUEZ. Not so bad.

DENNIS. But did it ever create, like, a conflict of interest? When you were on the beat in your old neighborhood?

RODRIGUEZ. What conflict of interest? I was glad to be where I grew up, people were glad to have me there, keeping things safe.

DENNIS. I didn't mean –

RODRIGUEZ. Forget it.

DENNIS. I'm sorry, I mean, I wasn't –

RODRIGUEZ. Let me get back to asking some questions, I've had enough sandwich here.

(**HE** *puts away the rest of it in the paper bag, wipes his hands with a napkin.*)

I'd like to get more of a sense of who your brother was close to.

DENNIS. He wasn't close to anyone.

RODRIGUEZ. I want you to tell me about Byron.

DENNIS. (*pretending not to understand what* **RODRIGUEZ** *means*) Byron was one of the great Romantic poets of the Nineteenth Century. His most famous work may be his novel in verse, *Don Juan*. Actually, the British would pronounce that Don Jew-in. Seriously.

RODRIGUEZ. Very nice. Now tell me about your brother's friend Byron.

DENNIS. My brother's friend Byron would have been happy to kill Michael to help him out, I'm sure. But he didn't have a key to our apartment.

RODRIGUEZ. Tell me about him anyway.

(**DENNIS** *is quiet for a long time. At last, he speaks.*)

DENNIS. That's the thing about Michael that alienated me the most. That I just could never understand. Why he became a homeless bum. I think some of it was from reading Orwell, *Down and Out in Paris and London*. When I was a kid, Michael told me how Orwell was raised to have this horror of poor people. He was always told that "the lower classes smell." And so when he left the Imperial Police in Burma, and stopped being a colonial officer with a bungalow and servants and all, he just dropped out, allowed himself to sink, so that he was a tramp or a hobo or whatever they called it, and suddenly he was living with those people, and soon he was smelling bad himself. And that was how he did penance for having served the Empire, and for being snobby toward poor people. So, maybe Michael got too into that idea, or read the book too many times. But, yeah. For years, my brother smelled.

RODRIGUEZ. And Byron?

DENNIS. Byron Carson is his best friend. Going back years.

RODRIGUEZ. Friend or lover?

DENNIS. I beg your pardon? Friend only, as far as I know.

RODRIGUEZ. Where did they meet?

DENNIS. They both lived for several years in Tompkin Square Park. In the tent city. I tried to visit with my brother there. I'd bring him food, he'd share it with Byron and the rest. I tried to get him to leave, to come to housing I'd arranged for. He said he had housing. I tried to get him to come to Mom and Dad's funerals, each time – and he wouldn't even leave for that. After the city tore the tents down – that's when I lost touch with him, for over a decade.

RODRIGUEZ. How do you and Byron get along?

DENNIS. We don't, really. He always seems to be laughing at me. Kind of like Michael.

RODRIGUEZ. Were you there the last time he and your brother saw each other?

DENNIS. Pretty much. Standing by. I was there when he arrived, and I frisked him before he got the chance to be alone with Michael. He couldn't have slipped him anything.

RODRIGUEZ. Tell me about it.

(*Lights come up on the apartment.* **MICHAEL** *is lying in his bed.* **DENNIS** *crosses into his apartment slowly, as he and* **RODRIGUEZ** *speak.*)

DENNIS. I had Byron wait in the vestibule, and I went in to "announce" his arrival to Michael. For once, Michael didn't seem so thrilled that Byron was there.

(*to* **MICHAEL**)

You want me to send him away?

MICHAEL. *(rubbing face)* Yes. No, but give me a minute.

DENNIS. Do you not feel well, Michael?

MICHAEL. I feel like shit, but that's a given. I'm just not quite sure that this is one of my "at home" days. That I am receiving visitors at this time.

DENNIS. I'd be glad to tell him to –

MICHAEL. Yeah, I'm sure you would. But we drive away my one and only friendly visitor, maybe he never bothers to come back. Just give me a minute, here.

(He tries to shift his weight. Then, he puts out an arm to ask for help, and DENNIS *helps him shift into something like a sitting position, plumping pillows behind him, to prop him up.)*

MICHAEL. *(cont.)* Shit.

DENNIS. What?

MICHAEL. Nothing. Just the knives in my back. Nothing a little more morphine couldn't cure.

DENNIS. Well, that's out, but if there's anything else I can help you –

MICHAEL. Is he bringing me anything? Anything you'll allow in your apartment?

DENNIS. I didn't see any packages on him.

MICHAEL. But you haven't groped him yet.

DENNIS. I haven't frisked him, no.

MICHAEL. You gonna stay and hang out with us? And radiate your pretty pink disapproval?

DENNIS. Not for long, Mike. Do you want to see Byron or not? Because if you don't, there's actually a lesson I could be preparing, and I'll tell him to leave, and then go off and do that.

MICHAEL. A lesson on what?

DENNIS. James Baldwin.

MICHAEL. "Sonny's Blues"?

DENNIS. Yeah.

MICHAEL. That's funny. Don't you think that's funny? I'd love to sit in your classroom and watch you teach it.

DENNIS. Do I let your friend in or do I tell him to leave?

MICHAEL. Bring him on. If he's ready for me, I'm ready for him.

(DENNIS goes to the door and undoes some of the locks, and lets BYRON into the apartment, calling out:)

DENNIS. Byron? We're open for business.

(BYRON CARSON enters the room, wearing an open flannel shirt over a soiled t-shirt, and pants that have not been washed in a while. He keeps his hands in the air, as though DENNIS has a gun on him.)

BYRON. Don't shoot. I'll cooperate. No funny stuff, I promise. Please, officer, be gentle with me.

DENNIS. Look, I'm not crazy for this, either.

(He goes to BYRON, who stands still, and pats him down.)

BYRON. Oh, come on now. You know you get off on this stuff.

MICHAEL. It's his favorite part of the day.

(DENNIS is squatting now, patting down BYRON's pants legs and and ankles.)

Don't forget the footwear. They might be packed with plastic explosives – You know about Byron's Al-Qaeda past, right? Keep your eyes peeled for a fuse.

(BYRON laughs at this. DENNIS stands.)

DENNIS. I don't think so. I think he's okay.

BYRON. I'm clean?

MICHAEL. Well, you're hardly clean, Byron, but you're free of contraband. Unless you'd like to do a thorough body cavity search, Dennis?

DENNIS. That won't be necessary.

BYRON. Damn. Just as I was getting into it.

DENNIS. *(to himself)* Why did I assume he was clean?

(He steps out of the scene, and addresses RODRIGUEZ, over in his office.)

DENNIS. *(cont.)* People like that think nothing of carrying drugs in any part of the body, places where I'd be embarrassed to pat him down. He *could* have smuggled anything in to Michael, and Michael just didn't use it till the next morning, for some reason.

RODRIGUEZ. Keep going.

DENNIS. *Why* did I assume he was clean? He could have done it.

RODRIGUEZ. What happened next?

MICHAEL. Dennis is preparing to teach a class on "Sonny's Blues." You know that story, Byron?

BYRON. Naw. What's it about?

MICHAEL. About a guy trying to save his tragic older brother, hooked on heroin.

DENNIS. His tragic younger brother.

MICHAEL. Oh yeah? I haven't read it for a while.

BYRON. Does he save him?

MICHAEL. No, but he learns to respect his alternate life-style choices.

DENNIS. Mock all you want, but it's a good story.

MICHAEL. Maybe so, but we'll see how much is left of it when you get through with it.

DENNIS. You've never seen me teach, you don't know if I'm any good.

MICHAEL. I'm sure you're inspiring.

BYRON. Now, go easy on the boy, Mike, he's your own brother.

MICHAEL. Byron's all heart. You know how I met him, Dennis? These brats from NYU Film School came by Tompkin Square, wanting to shoot footage of all of the guys living there. Dead of winter. This one earnest girl goes up to Byron, marches up and says, "Is it okay if I shoot you?" And Byron doesn't see she's got a camera crew of scared little boys behind her, terrified we'll rape them and steal their expensive equipment. He just thinks she's a crazy person who maybe has a gun. And he's soothing her, saying to her: "It's okay, baby.

It's gonna be all right. You don't have to shoot nobody, it's gonna be all right." And this girl just keeps asking him, "But is it okay if I shoot you?"

(He and **BYRON** *are laughing at this,* **DENNIS** *cracks a smile.)*

MICHAEL. *(cont.)* I said, this is a *prince* of a guy. This is a kitten rescuer, right here. And you know, he was the one the stray cats would always go to. Cats that wouldn't let anybody close to them, nobody else would *want* to get close to them, would wind up in his tent.

BYRON. Nothing like five cats to keep you from freezing your ass off sleeping in a tent in the middle of winter. Best heating system I know about.

MICHAEL. Cats with stuff crawling on their fur no entomologist has ever seen.

DENNIS. How did you – Byron, how did you wind up in Tompkin Square? I mean, Michael doesn't like to tell me how he…but I was just curious…

BYRON. You're thinking how does a smart, charming man like myself get homeless?

DENNIS. Well…

BYRON. Now, that's an interesting question. How does one man's life hit the fan? But I'm not sure you're exactly the right guy to hear the answer. You understand, Dennis? I'm not sure you could really "identify." And it might mess up this image your brother is giving you about me, that I help the stray cats and little girls that wander into the park.

DENNIS. If you don't want to –

BYRON. I was married. I had a wife, and a kid. A nice apartment. You'd be surprised. A good life. Some ignorant people think: you're born homeless, you've never lived on the other side. But plenty of guys live in society, go along thinking it's gonna be like that forever. Then, bam, it's all gone. Just like that. Damn, I had a thirty-inch TV, a sound system I was proud of. And I had a beautiful wife.

(pause)

And I loved that woman. Jesus. I never loved nobody that much, and I would have been right there for her till the day I died or she died, I would have been right there. And then I lose my job. And right away, I can see her respect for me going down. She couldn't even *see* me. I loved her for *her*, you understand what I am saying? Her love just start draining out of her, soon as I lose my job. She start seeing me as less than a man. And talking nasty about me to the kid, in this nasty tone of voice. And I go away with my buddies for a few days. Guy has a basement apartment, he's showin' kung fu movies, we just drunk and stupid, hangin' out for a weekend, nobody got a job, daddy Bush's recession, who the fuck cares, relax with the fellas for a little while. I get home. There is another man in the apartment with her. Another man sleeping with my wife – and maybe that was nothing new, and I was just blind before. But another man is in my home now, playing with my child. And my wife tells me the lease is in her name, I don't live there no more, she wants a divorce, I should just take my things and go back to my friend's place.

(He pauses, remembering.)

My wife had a beautiful smile, and she knew it, too. A mouth full of pearly white, perfect teeth. A Colgate smile. You'd think she was smiling to be warm, or 'cause she like you – she just showing off those teeth. Make fun of me with my yellow teeth. So, I take a look at her, and this piece of shit man she got living in my house all of a sudden, and I knock some of those beautiful teeth right out of her smile. And I mess up his smooth face, and break a couple of bones, and they press charges, and I ain't got no lawyer worth a damn. And I do some time, and then when I get out, I wind up in the park. With a bunch of other losers without a life. Who threw it away, or had it taken away. A place your brother used to call...

MICHAEL. The Island of Lost Boys.

BYRON. I had found a country that felt right to me, where I could belong. And when they closed down that country, I found me a subway train of my choice, and when they kick me off the train and it just get too cold, I wind up in the shelter. I been back to prison a few times, I don't mind it so much. I work out when I'm there, I get into shape. But the shelter ain't no place to be if you can help it. Does that answer your question?

MICHAEL. Mason still there?

BYRON. Naw, they kicked him out. He was acting psycho.

MICHAEL. What did he do to get kicked out?

BYRON. He get fucked up, shit-faced and high out of his mind, he start singing and rapping and talking to his-self, and staggering around and picking fights with people. He cut a guy for a pack of Marlboros not even his.

(to DENNIS)

You know, all this catching up and reunion stuff, it can't be so interesting for you.

MICHAEL. Don't worry about Christopher Robin. He gets off on it. He lives vicariously through our adventures.

DENNIS. Don't call me Christopher Robin. I'm just trying to get to know Byron a little better.

MICHAEL. Sorry, Bueller. Carry on.

BYRON. *(To MICHAEL)* But what I'm saying is, maybe you and I could use some time to talk and hang out without him getting off on it, or whatever he does when he's listening in.

MICHAEL. Aha. Dennis. Don't you have some sort of lesson plan to write? I believe you're going to go teach a class of some kind?

DENNIS. *(with sarcastic brightness)* You know what, I was just heading into my room.

BYRON. Couldn't you maybe take a hike for a while? Walk around the block?

DENNIS. I'm afraid not, Byron. And after all, this *is* my apartment.

BYRON. Yeah, that's the one thing my old lady taught me, and it really sank in. Love, trust, family, they're fine, whatever. But the person with the lease, that's the person who got everything.

MICHAEL. Slaves of New York.

DENNIS. Sorry to get in your way. If you want something to eat, Byron, there's left-over stir-fry in the fridge.

BYRON. *(with mock excitement)* Stir-fry! One of your vegetable stir-fries?

DENNIS. Yes, and there's a container of hummus, and crackers.

BYRON. But none for Michael?

DENNIS. None for Michael. It's too fattening. I hope you'll respect my wishes on this point.

BYRON. Oh, I got nothing but respect for you, man. This is your apartment.

(DENNIS goes into his room, irritated, slams the door.)

(Lights down over the apartment)

(DENNIS reappears in RODRIGUEZ's office, walking more slowly, contemplative and dazed.)

DENNIS. *(cont.)* I am such a fool. He could have slipped him something then. I opened the door to my room again, a crack. But I guess he could possibly have gone back to the vestibule, maybe he had something in his coat. Even with all the locks, I might not have heard him go in there –

RODRIGUEZ. How long did he stay?

DENNIS. Twenty minutes, I guess. Then I had to go to class, and I made him leave with me.

RODRIGUEZ. And this is all happening yesterday?

DENNIS. Yes.

RODRIGUEZ. And you have no idea what else went on between them, when you were in your room?

DENNIS. I think Michael gave him some stuff to mail. I think they were talking about guys they knew at the shelter, mostly. Gossiping. I heard them laughing. At times I heard them talking seriously. I was trying to concentrate on work.

RODRIGUEZ. Did you teach a good lesson?

DENNIS. No. I was distracted. It sucked.

(He rubs his face with his hand.)

RODRIGUEZ. You must be tired. Do you want a break?

DENNIS. No. This is something to do. I can't even think about – leaving this office. About going back there –

RODRIGUEZ. You'll take some time off. Go on a trip.

DENNIS. I can't, I teach.

(There is a knock at the door.)

RODRIGUEZ. Come.

*(The door opens, and **EDITH** enters.)*

Yes, may I help you?

DENNIS. *(looking up)* Edith?

EDITH. They told me you were in here, Dennis. They took me to the apartment to ask me questions, and I grabbed you this container of stir-fry, from the fridge.

DENNIS. Well, I'm not – but thanks. That was thoughtful.

(He takes the brown bag from her.)

RODRIGUEZ. Does Lieutenant Tanner know you're here, Ms. Singleton?

EDITH. He told me I had two minutes to bring the food in.

DENNIS. I guess you guys figure: question us separately, in different rooms, see if our stories match up, right?

RODRIGUEZ. We're taking the case seriously enough to have several officers involved.

EDITH. And they have Julie at the apartment now.

DENNIS. *(angry)* They're questioning Julie?

EDITH. They were bringing her in as they took me out of the building. They'll be bringing her here next.

DENNIS. *(to* **RODRIGUEZ**, *furious)* You are just not hearing a single goddamn word –

EDITH. Dennis, I think perhaps you ought to phone your solicitor. I have phoned mine.

DENNIS. Phone my...I don't have a lawyer. I hardly know any lawyers. Guys I went to college with – but we're not close.

EDITH. Then ask for the yellow pages, and find one. For you and for Julie.

RODRIGUEZ. No one is charged with anything yet.

EDITH. But we will be, soon. And I have been a nurse long enough to know that even when a man wants to die, and finds a way, the state feels they ought to blame someone, and sometimes they go after his caretakers. Think about it, Dennis. Dennis?

DENNIS. *(looking away)* I didn't do it, Edith. Did you?

EDITH. No, Dennis. I don't know how Michael managed. I only know that I am glad he finally found a way.

(to **RODRIGUEZ***)*

And you may write down on your pad that I said that, though no one has read me my rights yet, and my solicitor has not arrived.

(We hear someone calling to her from offstage.)

OFFSTAGE VOICE. Ms. Singleton?

EDITH. *(calling out door)* I'll be there in a moment.

(to **DENNIS***)*

Don't get too beaten down, Dennis. Call for some help. And don't beat yourself up too much, either. Don't begrudge Michael some peace at last.

(She goes. **DENNIS** *continues to look down.)*

DENNIS. I still can't tell. I still don't know for sure if she did it. You'd think I'd know, listening to her. And in one second I'm convinced she did, and the next...

RODRIGUEZ. Take me through your last conversation with Michael.

DENNIS. This morning?

RODRIGUEZ. This morning. Take me through everything that happened, from the moment you woke up.

*(Lights come up on the other side of the stage. **DENNIS** slowly makes his way over into that space, as he narrates to **RODRIGUEZ**.)*

DENNIS. I got up early. Six, maybe. Michael was still asleep, or it looked like he was. I took my shower. I made myself breakfast.

RODRIGUEZ. What did you make?

DENNIS. Scrambled eggs with onions and peppers. Michael claims – claimed the smell drove him crazy.

RODRIGUEZ. But there was none for him.

DENNIS. Eggs are so fattening, high cholesterol. His breakfast is a bran cereal with soy milk. I've told him that if he'll only agree to an exercise regimen, then breakfast will get better. The good smell is – you'd think it would be incentive.

RODRIGUEZ. You gave him his cereal?

DENNIS. Yes.

*(**HE** carries a bowl from the kitchen to **MICHAEL**, who is sitting up in bed.)*

He asked for some eggs. He's asked before, but – maybe more pointedly this morning. He said something like:

MICHAEL. *(mildly)* What if you came home, and I was no more, and you had denied me a last meal of scrambled eggs and onions? Could you live with yourself, if your last gastronomical act toward me were one of such utter pettiness and stinginess?

RODRIGUEZ. And?

DENNIS. Well, I didn't think anything of it. I mean, Michael talked of dying all the time, there were pretty strongly worded reproaches all the time, he whined about food a lot.

*(to **MICHAEL**)*

DENNIS. *(cont.)* I'd rather feed you a breakfast that won't hurt you, Mike, and come home to find you your usual cheerful self.

(realizing) But maybe this meant – of course he knew he was going to die.

RODRIGUEZ. But you didn't give him eggs.

DENNIS. No. I took the cereal away when he was done with it. He doesn't eat that much anymore.

(He does so – deposits the bowl offstage back in the kitchen area. He re-enters the main room of the apartment.)

But because he's so sedentary, and I guess his metabolism, he doesn't lose the weight.

RODRIGUEZ. And then?

DENNIS. And then I went into the vestibule.

(He does so, leaving the door partially open so we still hear him.)

And then I gave him the shot of insulin.

(He comes back out with both the insulin, and the paper cup with the morphine drink. He puts the cup on the floor.)

*(**MICHAEL** turns on his side to be injected, and studies **DENNIS** as he gives him the shot. He doesn't really flinch.)*

DENNIS *(cont.)* I've always been haunted by the idea… He used to shoot up so much…and he wasn't clean about needles, he's had bouts of hepatitis…sometimes I imagine like there's something bad in the needle. I hate injecting him.

RODRIGUEZ. But the insulin doses come pre-packaged?

DENNIS. In the cartridges, yes. They're tamper-proof.

*(**DENNIS** puts the empty on the floor. Picks up the cup.)*

RODRIGUEZ. And then you give him the morphine?

DENNIS. Yes.

RODRIGUEZ. Why not first thing? If he's in pain, if you're about to give him a shot...

DENNIS. *(staring at* **MICHAEL***)* It's like a treat I save for last, since he's cooperated with me and all. Michael was okay with that. I think he liked to savor it – like he said. Like a cigarette. He usually takes the cup from me and sips it.

(thinks)

But this morning...

MICHAEL. Pour the nectar into me, little brother.

DENNIS. What?

MICHAEL. Like a mama bird feeding a baby bird. I'll open my beak, with my eyes closed, and you bring on the love.

DENNIS. What is this, Mike?

MICHAEL. You never worked with a difficult child before? Make the choo choo train go down the hatch. Fly the airplane home!

(He closes his eyes, and opens his mouth. **DENNIS** *rolls his eyes, pours the drink into his mouth.)*

DENNIS. Well, I feel mildly ridiculous here, but – fine.

*(***MICHAEL** *smacks his lips, as* **DENNIS** *crumples the cup and throws it in a small trash can.* **MICHAEL***'s sigh is one of happiness.)*

MICHAEL. Crystal clear, like a waterfall. Nature's goodness.

DENNIS. I guess you could say that.

MICHAEL. The purest stuff on Earth. Of course, heroin can also run clear. When you cook it up.

DENNIS. Well, use your imagination.

MICHAEL. It's funny that none of them are quite as silky as methadone, though, and that one's entirely synthetic. You know what they say?

DENNIS. No, I don't, Mike.

MICHAEL. It was developed first in Nazi Germany. They named it Dolophine, after Adolph Hitler.

DENNIS. No kidding?

MICHAEL. But I've also heard that's a myth. That Dolophine was coined from "dolor," for pain, and "fin" for end. You could call any opiate that, couldn't you?

DENNIS. I guess.

MICHAEL. Even its older, more organic cousins. And we like to live organically in this household! We stick with the classics! Tried and tested...

DENNIS. I'm going to have to be heading in soon, Mike, so if there's anything –

MICHAEL. Whichever you choose, the pain ends, and you float away in the crystal clear, cool water.

DENNIS. I'm sorry if it clouds your thinking. But it doesn't preclude you from doing anything that you –

MICHAEL. *(singsong, as if reciting a primer lesson)* Of course, as we know, the most addictive drug of *all* is nicotine!

DENNIS. You up for a bathroom run, Mike?

MICHAEL. It's the highlight of my day. Having you there to supervise makes it so much more special. Like having Mom here to take care of me.

DENNIS. I don't have Mom's light touch.

MICHAEL. No. But you have the same attention to detail. And the same nervous – busy-ness. Very busy people. The same righteous air, that you're a *good person*. And you will suffer the follies and cruelties of the *bad* person with a weary martyr's resignation.

DENNIS. That's not how Mom saw you.

MICHAEL. Unshakeably righteous. Unshakeably smug.

DENNIS. I wish she'd loved me one *eighth* as much as she loved you. You were a god to her.

MICHAEL. So afraid of anything outside of convention, outside of the world of couch covers and *Reader's Digest.* If the unexamined life is not worth living, what do you call a life like that? Industrious busy-work in a vacuum. Hovering over the vacuum cleaner.

DENNIS. Have you examined your life, Michael?

MICHAEL. I have. And I must report that it is also not worth living. But Mom never examined hers. How she needed a rude bullying bastard like Socrates to grab her by the shoulders verbally and *shake* her!

DENNIS. You did your best, Michael. You were every bit as much of a bullying bastard as Socrates.

MICHAEL. That was the one viewpoint I remember you having, as a child. Instead of parroting what I said. I read you Socratic dialogues – and you said you hated Socrates.

DENNIS. Yeah.

MICHAEL. Can you remember why?

DENNIS. Because he took such sadistic pleasure in cornering people. Tripping them up, even after he'd won.

MICHAEL. Isn't it possible he was just trying to get them to examine their assumptions?

DENNIS. He said he was after knowledge, but he was just showing off and taking people apart.

MICHAEL. Oh, now, that's not a constructive attitude. If a smug, moralizing hypocrite is forced to think –

DENNIS. He was the smuggest of the bunch. He was out to destroy people's dignity. He was a public menace.

MICHAEL. Well, they certainly disposed of him as if he were.

(beat)

It's remarkable you still feel so strongly about it. That you hate outright the man who did the most to get people on planet Earth to look at themselves, to *think*, with both headlights on.

DENNIS. Yeah, the way you forced Mom to "think," right?

MICHAEL. *(getting a little bit dreamy)* Mmm. I tried. But all I ever did was make her feel wounded. Increase the martyr complex…

DENNIS. She was a good woman, and it would have meant a lot to her if you had come to Dad's funeral. Or hers.

MICHAEL. Well, you know what us Boomers say. "You can't always get what you want."

DENNIS. *(wheeling chair over)* Can we get this over with? I have to get to work.

(turns toward **RODRIGUEZ**, *takes a few steps toward him)*

I took him to the bathroom. Same as always. I put him back to bed, and put the chair out of reach.

(does so)

I didn't want him trying to climb into it while I was out, and hurting himself.

(puts on jacket, picks up briefcase)

And we had one more exchange before I left.

MICHAEL. Heading out into the world, little brother?

DENNIS. That's where I'm going.

MICHAEL. Tell it to kiss my ass.

DENNIS. I'll do that, Mike.

MICHAEL. *(languid)* I may not watch my talk shows today.

DENNIS. Oh no?

MICHAEL. I feel dreamy and peaceful and euphoric. I may just lie here and compose a play. Something simple and elegant and spare. Classical. Like *Oedipus*, or Albee's *Zoo Story*.

DENNIS. Would you like a notebook and pencil?

MICHAEL. No, that's all right. I'm going to compose it behind my eyelids. I'm going to compose it out of dreams.

DENNIS. *(uncertain, kind of happy)* Well – I'm really glad you're thinking of writing again. I'd love to hear about it when I get back. Are you sure you don't want a pen and –

MICHAEL. No means no, little brother. No means no. No means no.

DENNIS. I'm sorry. I just – hey, I guess I just want to be part of the artistic process.

MICHAEL. Don't worry, Dennis. You're a part of this play. You're already in it. I'm writing it for you. And me... I need your collaborative input.

(He seems to be drifting off. **DENNIS** *tucks in his blankets, around the sides, rather uncertain, but touched.)*

DENNIS. That's – that's really nice, Mike. We'll have a long talk when I get home, okay? Collaborating with you – would be an honor. I mean, two guys live together…it would be great if they could create something greater than the sum of the parts, you know? And we're brothers, we could –

MICHAEL. We've never touched each other, Dennis. Oh, you've held on to me while I take a crap. You've hauled my carcass all over. But your pep talks and sermons and good works…you've never touched me at all. It's only today that you have finally done something.

DENNIS. *(confused)* I have?

MICHAEL. *(eyes closed, dreamy)* You have finally accomplished something. You've touched me. And by changing my life, perhaps you can transform your own.

DENNIS. *(laughs nervously)* You're getting cryptic on me, Mike. You're losing me.

MICHAEL. Well, then, goodbye, little brother.

(Eyes still closed, he gives a little wave. **DENNIS** *picks up his briefcase, heads for the door, pauses and looks back at* **MICHAEL**. *He addresses* **RODRIGUEZ**.*)*

DENNIS. That was how I left him. And that was how I found him. Except when I found him, his lips were white with foam.

(There is a knock at the door of **RODRIGUEZ**'s *office.)*

RODRIGUEZ. Come.

*(***JULIE** *enters, wearing a long coat.)*

You must be Julie.

JULIE. Yes.

*(***DENNIS** *focuses on her, sees her.)*

DENNIS. Honey?

*(***HE** *rushes over into the other scene, in* **RODRIGUEZ**'s

office. He and **JULIE** *embrace for a long moment.)*

They giving you a hard time?

JULIE. Uh uh. It's okay.

DENNIS. You hadn't seen Michael for ages!

JULIE. I know, I told them. It's okay, Dennis.

(a beat)

How you holding up?

DENNIS. I'm – you know, I'm a zombie. So, there are advantages to that.

JULIE. Edith thinks we should –

DENNIS. A lawyer. Right.

JULIE. I've called one. He's on his way down. If it gets weird for you – just stop. If it feels wrong for any reason. Just stop answering questions until this guy gets here. Okay?

DENNIS. I want to find out who killed him.

JULIE. He killed himself.

DENNIS. He had help. Some contemptible bastard helped the smartest, boldest, most remarkable person on planet Earth slip out between the cracks, just when he was about to accomplish something, just when he was thinking of writing something new. And I want to know who it was. My curse on that fucking bastard's head –

JULIE. Dennis, what is the point of –

DENNIS. I want to know.

JULIE. Okay, sweetie. Okay.

DENNIS. They start questioning you, yet?

JULIE. When I get out of here. They're still looking for Byron – he's a little harder to find.

DENNIS. Yeah, I'll bet. I'm just…

JULIE. *(to cheer him)* Here, they let me bring you your mail.

DENNIS. How did you get at my mail?

JULIE. You gave me keys to your door and your mailbox, remember? In case you went on a trip? I have them on the same chain.

DENNIS. I don't remember that.

JULIE. *(reaches into pocket, producing one slim letter)* The junk mail I left. But this looked like real mail, from a real person. No return address, but –

DENNIS. Give me that.

(He takes the letter and looks at it, very upset.)

JULIE. You know who it's from?

DENNIS. It's from Michael. That's his handwriting. I haven't seen it for years.

JULIE. How could Michael –

DENNIS. He must have given it to Byron to mail. Maybe while I was out of the room. Maybe he wrote it then.

RODRIGUEZ. Yesterday?

DENNIS. Yes. And Byron mailed it right away. And the good old New York postal service delivered it today.

RODRIGUEZ. *(putting out his hand)* May I see that?

DENNIS. *(holding it protectively)* No. It's my letter.

RODRIGUEZ. Why don't you open it, then?

*(**JULIE** and **RODRIGUEZ** stare at **DENNIS** expectantly. He turns away from them and carefully opens the envelope. He extracts a small square of paper, densely covered with writing. He glances at them, then reads aloud:)*

*(Note: It's also possible to bring lights up on **MICHAEL**, in bed or in his chair, and have him deliver this speech, then become a corpse again for the rest of the play. His voice can overlap with **DENNIS'** at some point in the course of the letter, and then deliver the rest of it alone.)*

DENNIS. Dear Baby Brother, Hopefully, I will be gone when you receive this. Thank you for giving Byron some time alone in the vestibule, before he joined me. Thank you for allowing me a bit of time to compose this now. Thank you for the ministrations I look forward to, tomorrow morning, when you will allow me to sip at the nectar that will set me free.

(He registers the implications of this. Looks up. Looks

around, confused. **JULIE** *takes a step toward him.)*

JULIE. Dennis –

DENNIS. *(reading again)* Byron says there wasn't much left in the cannister of morphine punch, and perhaps he has added enough crystal clear liquid H to pack a wallop. He's cool with me saying it was he who mixed the punch, but then again, perhaps these are only the scribbled ravings of a burned-out madman, implicating his friend for no reason. And after all, it will be you that gives it to me, and can you really say for sure that this is not what you've wanted? Thank you for all your assiduous care and concern, which makes me so confident you will administer freedom to me in the morning, and which makes it so easy for me to get the hell away from you, and use you in this constructive manner. As you read this, I am far, far away, where a bum can stay for many a day, amidst the buzzing of the bees in the cigarette trees. Now that you've murdered the dreary, worn-out goblin hanging over your life, as you needed to do all along, maybe you will think. Harder. Maybe you will get a life of your own. So long, Sucker…

JULIE. Dennis, put it down.

DENNIS. Michael.

JULIE. Put it down. Give it to the man. It's evidence that you had no idea. No idea what he and Byron were up to.

DENNIS. He wanted it to be by my hand. Not anybody else's.

RODRIGUEZ. I agree with her, Mr. Kadman. I don't think any legal charge will come from this. There's no case. Maybe against his friend, but not against you.

(He takes the letter. **DENNIS** *wanders away from them, into his apartment: the room where* **MICHAEL** *'s body still lies.* **RODRIGUEZ** *turns to* **JULIE***.)*

RODRIGUEZ *(cont.)* And I think we can conclude our investigation. That's how it looks right now. I'll tell the officers who were talking to you and Edith.

(He goes out. DENNIS *sits on the bed beside* MICHAEL*'s corpse.)*

DENNIS. You didn't want anyone else to do it. This was the play you wanted to write. It's good to see you finally complete a project, Michael. A lot of forethought and planning and stick-with-it-ness went into this. It makes me proud.

JULIE. *(calls over to him)* Dennis?

DENNIS. *(to* MICHAEL*)* I came in and saw you with the foam on your lips. And tried to tell myself that you were sleeping. But I knew. I knew right away. It's not you anymore. Just an ugly old house, with nobody home. A fat bag of bones. They can burn it, bury it, I don't care what they do with it. You're gone, your mind, your mind. And I'm more alone than I was during all the years you were gone. I'm all alone, for real.

*(*RODRIGUEZ *re-enters his office. He speaks to* JULIE*.)*

RODRIGUEZ. The other officers agree, I showed them the letter. I mean, we may want to check the handwriting, make sure it's his brother's. Compare it to his. But assuming it all checks out…We'll be closing the investigation.

JULIE. I'd be glad to answer any –

RODRIGUEZ. We have everything we need for now. There are doctors we'll be speaking to. But you people can go home.

JULIE. *(indicating* DENNIS*)* I'm worried about him, he's really zoning out.

RODRIGUEZ. He needs some therapy to work through this. Whatever guilt his brother wanted him to feel, and it seems like Michael laid it on pretty thick, by choosing this way…a good therapist will know how to help.

DENNIS. *(to* MICHAEL*)* You know, when I moved you in, I kind of wanted to move my bed out here, to be across the room from yours. Like when we were little, and I was in my crib, and then my cot, and you were across the room, on your bed. And you'd read to me, and talk with me, and then after Mom shut out the light, you'd whisper to me, and recite. And I used to drift off to the sound of your voice. I think I was the happiest baby in the whole world. And when you were a shit to me later, when you wouldn't talk, when you'd play those mind-fucking games, I'd still remember that. Being a baby, and drifting off to that voice. I'd think: this is not my brother. This is an impostor damaged by drugs. But then sometimes, my brother would peep through at me. And then I'd realize: that was one of the mind-fuck games.

JULIE. Dennis, you can stay at my place this week. I'll go back to yours and get your things, just tell me what you need.

DENNIS. You'd say: "I'll hold the ball, Charlie Brown, and you come running up and kick it!" Like Lucy. And I'd fall for it. I'd go flying, and land on my ass, every time. And then when you'd disappear, and Mom would be staggering around the house, hysterical – I could never touch anything in the room. It was never really my room, always yours. I couldn't sleep in your bed. They wouldn't have wanted that. And I didn't question it. I didn't want to disturb the shrine. All through high school, when you were long gone, I just wandered in the ruins of your world. I'd pick up notebooks, old DC comic books off the shelf, looking for clues. Pogo. I killed myself trying to read Pogo. *MAD* magazine books. Peanuts books. Books full of Crumb art. Kerouac and Camus and Burroughs. And I'd try to complete the process you'd started, of shaping me. I threw myself into causes and ideas you'd discarded long ago. I wanted to be good enough, I wanted to understand enough so that you'd come back and be proud of me.

JULIE. Dennis, sweetheart, it's time to go now. My car's right outside.

DENNIS. Fuck you for walking out on me, again and again and again. Fuck you for snatching that football away. I wanted to kill you so many times. I never would have done it. I never would have hurt you. Fuck you for tricking me into doing it.

(JULIE *peers into the space of the other room, and gently touches his arm.*)

JULIE. Baby? It's gonna be okay.

RODRIGUEZ. If his nerves are shot, see this doctor. He can maybe just give him some pills to get through the next few days.

(*He scribbles a name and number on a piece of paper and gives it to her.*)

I'm really sorry about all this. It's times like this you want to be alone with grief and each other. I'm sorry the law has to be involved – it's just the way it goes.

JULIE. Sure. Thank you.

RODRIGUEZ. Take it easy.

(*He touches her on the arm, glances over at* DENNIS, *and leaves his office.* JULIE *steps out of his office, approaches* DENNIS *in the apartment.*)

DENNIS. (*to* MICHAEL) I'm numb now, and I'll be walking around with them, and interacting with them, and I'll always be right in here with you now. That's all I'll see. This is where I'm going to stay. I'm as damaged as you are now, as damaged as you wanted me to be.

JULIE. We're getting out of here, Dennis, it's bad, it feels like a prison.

DENNIS. I'm all dammed up, my borders are closed, and she can't touch me anymore, nobody can touch me. I'm here with you. And you're gone. And I'm glad you chose me. It was my job. It didn't belong to anybody else.

JULIE. Come on, baby, we're going home now. It's okay. We're going home.

(She leads a zombie-like **DENNIS** *across from the apartment back into the office, as he stares ahead, not really seeing, and guides him through* **RODRIGUEZ**'s *office door.)*

(All lights go down, except for one over the body of **MICHAEL**. *Then, that goes out, too.)*

(Lights down)

End of Play

PROPS/SET/SOUND/COSTUME
NOTES

There must be a wheelchair for Michael, and ideally a bed as well, in the set comprising the main room of Dennis' apartment, which dominates the stage. A blanket will cover Michael's lap. There should be at least one window, with window bars on it to thwart thieves (and perhaps potential jumpers - perhaps when Dennis closes the window and swings the grillwork back in place, he locks it.). There should be some books and notebooks and a pile of papers, and a TV for Michael to watch, though we never see it on. Julie brings a houseplant. Dennis has an academic journal, a checkbook, and a piece of paper with an engagement ring taped to it. There is a door leading out to the vestibule and the front door, with many locks on it. There is another door to the bathroom, and one to Dennis' bedroom - or at least a specific exit leads to Dennis' bedroom, and another to the kitchen. Dennis wields a broom and dustpan at one point, and brings a cereal bowl and spoon, an insulin cartridge and a paper cup in toward the end. There is a small wastepaper basket.

The set for Rodriguez's office is also onstage throughout, and it should include a desk with two chairs, at least one framed picture, and a name plate for "T. Rodriguez." Rodriguez brings a sandwich in a bag. Edith brings a brown paper bag of food for Dennis. Julie brings in a letter in an envelope.

Sound effects include bathtub splashing and a doorbell. Costumes may include a nurse's uniform for Edith, nice clothes on Dennis and Julie for their date, more casual clothes for them the rest of the time, worn clothes on Byron and Michael, and a policeman's uniform for Rodriguez.

See what people are saying about
CELL...

"These days, when far too many authors of mystery and suspense give us cardboard characters in contrived situations and avoid anything with a social conscience, Judy Klass's *Cell* gives us believable dialogue about two brothers who are struggling with their own shortcomings and the social injustices that surround them–characters who live and breathe, needle and provoke, and who truly get under your skin."
- Kenneth Wishnia, Judge,
Best Play 2009 Edgar Allan Poe Awards,
Edgar-nominated author of *The Fifth Servant*

"*Cell* by Judy Klass is so much more than a taut mystery play. It is both reminiscent of Agatha Christie's whodunits and Gabriel Garcia Marquez's use of magical realism to capture characters, time, and place. Ms. Klass tells us at the play's beginning that her main character, Michael, has been murdered. Her taut and spellbinding play keeps its audience at the edge of their seats, guessing, waiting for the explosive ending."
- Woodie King Jr.,
Producing Director, *New Federal Theatre*

"*Cell* is the best new play I have presented since the Mystery Festival began. It is also very 'produceable' with great leading roles, small cast and a simple set – a producer's dream!"
- Zev Buffman,
president and CEO of RiverPark Center,
creator of the International Mystery Writers' Festival

OTHER TITLES AVAILABLE FROM SAMUEL FRENCH

THE FINAL TOAST
Stuart Kaminsky

Mystery Drama

7m (one teen), 2f

Unit Set

Winner of the 2008 Angie Award for Playwrighting!

The Edgar Prize-winning author Kaminsky tells the tale of one of literature's most famous detectives: Sherlock Holmes. In a witty, imaginative story filled with twists and unexpected surprises, Detective Holmes unravels a murder only to find himself the unwilling target of the killer-at-large. Along with the aid of his loyal and inquisitive companion, Dr. Watson, Sherlock Holmes uses his masterful power of deduction to make a nebulous situation seem "simply elementary." The Final Toast is an exciting new take on the classic characters of fiction we know and love, and its ending will please even the most savvy mystery connoisseurs.